The Truth about Earth, the Universe, the Spirit World

IRH Press

Originally published in Japan
as *El Cantare Jinsei no Gimon Nayami ni Kotaeru - Chikyu Uchu Reikai no Shinjitsu*
by IRH Press Co., Ltd., in March 2022.

BOOKS
IRH PRESS
New York

ISBN: 978-1-958655-26-9

Printed in Canada

First Edition

LIFE'S Q&A
with
EL CANTARE

The Truth about Earth, the Universe, the Spirit World

RYUHO OKAWA

IRH Press

Contents

Preface 13

CHAPTER ONE

The Development of Humans, Animals, and Plants

1 Debunking the Theory that Humans Evolved From Apes

My question to people who believe that humans evolved from apes 17

The apes of ancient times were regressed human souls 19

Thinking rationally about the origin of life 21

No one has been able to prove that spirits and the Spirit World do not exist 24

2 Spiritual Training for Plants

Plant souls have a mission and they each have a different state of mind 27

Be grateful to all existences that have a soul and are accomplishing their mission 30

3 The Secret behind the Souls of Animals, Plants, and Minerals

Plants may have a more refined vibration than humans do ... 33

Even animal spirits go to either heaven or hell after death 34

What do plants and animals think of the current age? 36

How do animal souls evolve into human souls? 37

Some animal spirits can speak human words 39

Plants exist in the spiritual world 42

Minerals have souls and are going through very slow soul training during their long lives 43

4 What Happens to Human Souls after Death?

The human spirit is made up of multiple entities 48

What does it mean to evolve spiritually? 50

CHAPTER TWO

The Earthly World, the Spirit World, and Hell

1 Right View in a World of Abundance

Why do religions often deny material objects? 54

Discover greater love by gaining the true worldview 57

2 The Power of Light That Is Creating This World

All things are created from attributes of light 61

3 How Was the Spirit World Created?

How the dimensional structure was built on Earth 64

How the living space for spirits in the other world was created 66

The Genesis of the Spirit World is a highly advanced teaching that is part of the Laws of El Cantare 67

4 The Difference between Evil Spirits in the Abysmal Hell and Satans

What turns a spirit into a satan are long years in hell and strong willpower 70

5 Why Did Darwin Fall to Hell?

The dangers of spreading harmful thinking by teaching a mistaken philosophy.. 73

How can Darwin and Marx be saved? 77

CHAPTER THREE

Eternal Life and Life Training

1 The Meaning of Suffering

Two ways of dealing with suffering 82

Relative dualism: why God allows suffering to exist 85

2 The Meaning of Death

Each person has their own destiny 89

3 How to Effectively Study and Practice the Truth in the Time You Have Remaining

The importance of accomplishing what you can in this life ... 92

4 The Problem with Thinking That "A Cause Is Immediately Followed by a Result"

Inga refers to "cause and effect" whereas *in'nen* refers to "cause and condition" 94

To achieve a result, you must not ignore the effort 95

5 How to Convey the Truth to Atheists

Be understanding toward people who have yet to awaken to the Truth 99

Consider whether it is the right time for the other person ... 101

Be mindful of how strongly the person is in need of the Truth 102

6 Life Training for Bodhisattvas-to-be

The difference between a hearer, a solitary realizer, and an arhat 106

How to become a true bodhisattva 108

7 How to Attain the State of Absolute Love

Consider yourself a part of God's Work 113

8 The Mindset to Have in an Age of Crisis

Always stick to Invincible Thinking 116

CHAPTER FOUR

The Reality of the Great Universe and Time from the Perspective of God

1 The Transformation of Planets into Black Holes as Seen by God

Considering a planet as a single life form 120

2 The Effect That Other Planets Have on Earth

A planet is born in one of three ways 124

The lessons learned from soul training on other planets affect the evolution of Earth 126

3 The Secret of Time Created by God

Time flows differently depending on your soul training environment 130

The power that allows the universe to exist is embedded in time 132

4 The Wonders of Time in the Other World

In the other world, time is not measurable with a clock 134

Only "the order of events" and "the chain of cause and effect" exist in the other world 136

5 Could You Travel Back in Time in a Time Machine and Change the Past?

There are limits to what people from the future can do in the past 139

CHAPTER FIVE

Understanding the Love and Mercy of God and Buddha

1 The Mistaken Claims Made by Buddhist Scholars Regarding Shakyamuni Buddha

How the Buddhist scholars view Shakyamuni 144

Shakyamuni taught the teachings that a person needed the most 146

2 The Truth about the Seven Buddhas of the Past

Buddha's past lives in the Jataka Tales: true or false? 149

3 Hermes' Love and Jesus' Love with Respect to the Developmental Stages of Love

Love itself is universal, but the difference lies in the viewpoint from which love is taught 152

4 Hermes' Teachings that Zeus Inherited

Zeus inherited the spirit of freedom and encouraged each individual to develop their talents 155

5 King Croud of the Ancient Incan Empire and His Involvement with Space Beings

King Croud rejected the mass immigration of space beings to Earth 157

6 Awakening to the Great Love of God

Not offering the Truth to people who are lost is a sin on our half 160

Plant the seeds of Truth in return for the love you received 162

Afterword 165

About the Author 169

Books by Ryuho Okawa 170

Who Is El Cantare? 180

About Happy Science 182

Happy Science's English Sutra 184

Memberships 185

Contact Information 186

About Happiness Realization Party 188

Happy Science Academy Junior and Senior High School 189

Happy Science University 190

About IRH Press USA Inc. 192

Preface

This seventh volume may be the last of the Q&A session series taken from my early lectures. At these lecture events, I gave an hour-long lecture, immediately followed by another hour of Q&A session, to several thousand or sometimes tens of thousands of people. As I reread this manuscript, I found that many of the questions I had been asked were of high level, to which I do not think any other religious leader would be able to give straight answers.

In this particular book, many questions revolved around science and physics. Speaking of the sciences, I—along with Newton, Einstein, and Professor Yukawa in the Real World—recently gave a lecture on the black hole equation at a place called Shambhala, a training center to pass down sacred spiritual rituals.

Although these Q&As were taken from my lectures given in the early years of Happy Science, I believe you will be able to grasp the deep philosophy behind my answers.

Ryuho Okawa
Master & CEO of Happy Science Group
February 11, 2022

CHAPTER ONE

The Development of Humans, Animals, and Plants

1

Debunking the Theory that Humans Evolved From Apes

Q1

I have a question about the theory of evolution, which is one of the bases of materialistic thinking.

Materialists believe that humans evolved from apes based on tangible facts like the discovery of the remains of apes and homo erectus fossils. Could you tell me what these beings truly looked like? Also, Happy Science teaches that humans have existed since prehistoric times, but for some reason, we have only discovered fossils of beings that seem to be on their way from apes to humans; we have not discovered any human fossils from prehistoric times. Could this be because of a negative spiritual influence? I would really appreciate it if you could put an end to the materialistic idea known as the "theory of evolution," once and for all.

Weekday Seminar A: Invincible Thinking (4), "The Power of Invincible Thinking"
Held on July 20, 1989 at Social & Cultural Hall in Tokyo, Japan

My question to people who believe that humans evolved from apes

Wow, you are giving off a very stiff vibration. You may have some "inflexible thinking" in you. I became a little stiff myself while I was listening to your question.

Actually, I have a question for those who believe in the theory of evolution. They say that humans evolved from apes, but if that's the case, why are apes still apes? Why do they still take the same form even though they've supposedly evolved into humans? They say that amphibians evolved from fish, but why, then, are fish still fish and amphibians still amphibians? Why are reptiles still reptiles? They say that "fishes evolved into birds and are now flying in the sky," but flying fish are still flying fish; it doesn't look like they'll be evolving into birds anytime soon. How do they explain that?

People make various claims based on old fossils, but if the theory of evolution is true, there should be some creatures that are evolving right now. So please tell me, at this very moment, which creatures are changing into different creatures? Please show me an ape that is about to become a human. We should be able to find examples of creatures that are evolving right now.

While it may take tens or hundreds of thousands of years for an ape to become a human, if the theory of evolution is true, we must be able to find one that is currently transitioning somewhere on Earth. But we see no such creatures. Nor do we see any organisms that are half-amphibian and half-reptile. There are no life forms that are undergoing change at this moment; they are all fully developed creatures. This is because there is a spiritual concept behind each creature that gives it its form. Currently, there are no creatures that are in the midst of transitioning.

Although it is said that there are no human fossils that are older than the fossils of apes, we need to take into account how many humans there actually were at that time. The current world population is at several billion, but if we go back 2,000 years, it may have only been around 300 million. Although there are no records to confirm it, I'm sure that's about it. If we go even further back in time, the number is probably much smaller.

What's more, many continents have risen from the ocean and sunk into the ocean throughout history, so it is rare for human remains to be preserved. It would be a miracle if any human remains were preserved after a continent sunk into the ocean. Also, it would help if human bones were made of non-perishable material that allowed them to remain perfectly intact, but that is not the case; rather, they disappear over time. The same goes for all other parts of the physical body. That is why it is extremely lucky to find fossils to begin with. For fossils to be discovered, the land they are on must not have sunk into the ocean or risen to form highlands, and they must be located in an area that is detectable by humans. In addition, the remains must have been buried suddenly or hardened quickly in some way, otherwise, they wouldn't have been preserved.

That is why I think it is unscientific for people to say that humans did not exist long ago just because they can't find the evidence. If they want to make this claim, they should dig up the entire Earth first.

The apes of ancient times were regressed human souls

Now, let me answer your other question about what apes were like in ancient times. As an example, I will refer to the Neanderthals who supposedly lived in ancient times. People who have examined their fossils say that, although their brains were bigger than that of humans, they did not have the same thinking abilities that humans did.

The truth is, these creatures were certainly not evolving to become human, but rather quite the opposite. Their souls were regressing. Essentially, human souls were evolving, but some of them were regressing. Let me use a river as an example. A river does not just flow in one direction, but there is also backflow, such as a whirlpool or an eddy. In the same way, it makes more sense to think that not all humans were evolving and that some were regressing. So, it isn't strange to find regressed souls. When these souls were born on earth, they expressed themselves in the form of ape-like creatures, who were slightly more intelligent than monkeys, and underwent spiritual training. In fact, this kind of thing did not just happen in the past—it is still ongoing today. For instance, it is said that an ape-like creature called the Yeti lives in the deep inland of China around the Himalayas. Apparently, it is eight to ten feet tall. Creatures like that are not on a path of evolution; rather, they are the result of human regression.

Some regressed human souls have difficulty finding a place to be born on earth. When they do and are born in places like tropical regions, they could become cannibals. Human souls that have regressed even further will dwell in animals like gorillas. Some of those who reside in gorilla bodies gradually transform and appear as half gorilla, half human. Beings like this exist. Inside those bodies are human souls. Although they were originally human, they cannot dwell in a human body because the wavelength of their minds is no longer in tune with it. There is a small percentage of souls like this.

So, please do not think that humanity has only ever made progress. Throughout history, humans have made progress but they have also regressed and stagnated. They have gone through all kinds of phases. Please think in this way and tell others about it.

Thinking rationally about the origin of life

Going back to your question about materialism, there is something that I would particularly like to point out. Simply put, the biggest and most fundamental issue with materialism is that it cannot explain why simple living organisms would develop the ability to think. Materialists use various theories including natural selection to explain how simple organisms developed into humans by coincidence. They say that amoeba-like organisms started moving around and eventually evolved into humans. Sure, there are small proteins that move around like amoebas. But why would these simple organisms need to become human? I would like to hear their answers to that.

Just consider the difference in the level of function between humans and amoebas—it is huge. Saying that amoebas became human is like saying that you sprinkled iron sand on the ground, left it there, and before you knew it, it turned into a computer. It's quite ridiculous. If despite developing into our current size, human beings today were simply eating food through our mouths, excreting waste through our anuses, and slithering around aimlessly like worms, then you could say that we have just developed from simple organisms and grown big over time. But that doesn't reflect reality because human beings can think creatively and I'm sure everyone would agree. I would like materialists to explain why humans became capable of thinking in this way.

To me, this is what materialism sounds like: "Once upon a time, there was a heap of sand. There was also a limestone that had been ground into powder. For some reason, there were also bricks and a plastering trowel lying on the ground. Then, it happened to rain, and for some reason, as it rained and the wind blew, cement was made, which turned into mortar. Then, suddenly, bricks flew up, mortar was applied to them, and they were all stacked up. Out of the blue, a roof was made, and before long, a house appeared out of nowhere."

However, that is not what you see if you observe nature. If you leave things be and let nature take its course, they will deteriorate. For example, what happens to a beautiful flower if you leave it be? It will wither. What happens after that? The petals will fall off. The flower then turns yellowish, and after that, it crumbles as its cells break down. In the end, it turns into soil. This is nature. If you let things be, everything will fade away and all things will lose their shape and form. You (the questioner) will also be broken down by ants if you lay down outside and let nature take its course. You will disintegrate and lose all shape and form. That is how nature works.

So, you can see how absurd it is to believe that evolution occurs on its own if nature is allowed to run its course. This is akin to thinking that basic materials, like sand, can develop intelligence on their own and build things like computers. The people who believe this are the ones with blind faith. If they can believe in something like that, they should also be able to believe in God. For things to appear out of the blue, there must be something that is enabling them to appear. Therefore, I believe it is much more rational to think that there is a *will* that intended to create humans as humans, monkeys as monkeys, and fish as fish, and that this *will* dwells within each creature as a life force and gives it its unique qualities.

No one has been able to prove that spirits and the Spirit World do not exist

Here is another point I want to make. Although many people say they do not believe in the spiritual world, I don't think anyone has successfully proved that spirits do not exist to this day. People have claimed that spirits do not exist but no one has succeeded in proving it.

On the contrary, countless people, I mean many, have provided proof that spirits, the Spirit World, and spiritual power exist. And yet, no one has proved that the Spirit World does not exist.

So, you can debate with materialists logically by saying, "If you believe in materialism, then prove to me that the material world is all that exists. Explain to me how the spiritual world does not exist." Since no one has been able to successfully explain it, they will eventually say, "I just believe it." You can then tell them, "But that is called faith." If they say that they simply believe in it, believe in how they feel, or only believe in what they have seen with their own eyes, then you can tell them, "That is the same as having faith." Although they cannot prove that the world they see is the same as the world you see, they *believe* that their worldview is right. So you should tell them, "What you are saying is also called faith."

I have spoken about a lot of things, but the point I am making is that living creatures are anything but simple. As I have illustrated in the example of a house I used earlier, a house won't get built through a series of coincidences. The materials to build a house already exist—if you go to the mountains, you can get trees, stones, and water. But a house will not magically build itself. This is the case for a simple building like a house but is even more so for humans. There is no way a human being with complex functions and thinking abilities could appear out of random coincidence.

Tiny life forms such as microorganisms can be made from proteins, but how can people conclude that they are not under some kind of spiritual influence? People say that these microorganisms suddenly move on their own, but in reality, many souls of microorganisms are floating in the air. For example, you may see an experiment where microorganisms similar to amoebas are made from proteins. They may then start moving, but that is because they are being influenced spiritually. So materialists should not be satisfied with seeing them move and think that it proves their theory. Rather, what they need to do is prove that there is no spiritual influence involved. Can they create a space where no spirit can get in? They cannot; it is impossible. A protein only starts moving when a spirit enters it. There is something that is affecting it.

So, if you want to debate logically with materialists, you should ask them for proof as well. Tell them, "Show me a creature that is currently transitioning to become a human, a chicken, or a fish." There are no such creatures. Despite this, evolutionists may still argue by referring to transitional fossils. But the truth is that all of the species were in complete form. For instance, there used to be a primal bird species called the archaeopteryx. People claim that the current bird species evolved from it, but there were no creatures in between the archaeopteryx and the current birds. If the current birds truly developed from the archaeopteryx, it would be possible to dig up many fossils that show this process of change. But that is not the case. There are always gaps in the fossil record.

Given all of this, you should adopt the idea that a change in the concept of a life form, along with other spiritual causes, led to an abrupt change to a creature or created a new creature.

I may not have put an end to materialistic thought once and for all, but I hope you can handle it from here.

2
Spiritual Training for Plants

Q2

We know that plants also have souls and that they comfort us in various ways by growing flowers and other things. Do plant souls undergo spiritual training repeatedly like us human beings and do they go to other planets for spiritual training? Also, if there is something we can do for these plants that give us all kinds of love, please let us know.

The Ninth Grand Public Lecture of 1990, "The Enlightenment of the Great Universe"
Held on August 26, 1990 at Makuhari Messe in Chiba, Japan

Plant souls have a mission and they each have a different state of mind

OK. Plant souls also go through the cycle of reincarnation on different planets. When a planet no longer has a suitable environment for plants to thrive in, plants cannot continue their soul training there. That is when they "close up shop," although that might not be an appropriate way to describe it. When plants cannot be born on a certain planet anymore, all of their souls come together and their human guiding spirits bring them to another planet. They do this at the same time that the human souls move to another planet. In this way, plant souls also go through reincarnation on various planets.

When it comes to a plant's mind, they have basic minds. The level of their minds varies, but they are all intelligent enough to understand about 300 words. They cannot show their responses because they do not have the organs to do so, but they have the intelligence to cover about 300 words. So, plants essentially have the intelligence level of a two- or three-year-old child.

Plants respond to all of the thoughts that humans have around them. Countless scientific experiments have been conducted on this in the past. For example, there were experiments with cacti and other plants to see what would happen if people held destructive thoughts toward them. In one experiment, the plants were attached to a polygraph instrument to measure their response. Just as their leaves were about to be harmed with a razor, they showed a sharp response, which meant that they were aware of what was coming. What's more, when music was played to them, the plants clearly emitted different vibrations depending on whether the music was peaceful or not. These experiments showed that plants have minds that can understand different vibrations.

To describe it more accurately, plants have souls that appear in a form similar to that of small human beings. Even flowers and trees have souls that look like young children. In old folklore, the spirits of nature are often depicted as fairies, and that is indeed what they look like. Such plant souls really do exist.

The main mission of plant souls is to create an environment. They create an environment suitable for advanced life forms to live and polish their souls in. One way plants do this is by sacrificing themselves; they help humans and animals grow by becoming their food. Another way is by creating beautiful scenery or a beautiful landscape, thereby expressing the elegance of their souls. Each plant will develop a different state of mind as a result of these actions. Plants with a more advanced state of mind reside in the Bodhisattva Realm and the Tathagata Realm. The Bodhisattva Realm and the Tathagata Realm are worlds where highly evolved human spirits reside. You will see that flowers also bloom in those realms. This means that some flowers possess a high level of consciousness equivalent to the human spirits living there.

On planet Earth, flowers bloom in all kinds of places. Although humans do not realize, flower souls have leaders. These flower soul leaders have advanced consciousness and reside in the realms of highly evolved human spirits. Of course, plants cannot move freely like human beings do and the actions they can take are limited. Even so, they have a highly advanced state of mind. You can see this, for example, by observing the flowers in the Shinshu area during summer. When you go there and see the flowers blooming everywhere, it makes you feel like you are in heaven. For flowers, the main consideration for their spiritual training is choosing where they will bloom on earth. If a flower decides to grow in an area with a lot of human activities, it could either advance or regress greatly. So, an urban area has a dramatic effect on plants. For example, if a flower is taken care of by someone who loves flowers, and is watered, talked to, and nurtured every day, it may develop to the level where it acquires human-like emotions. This will most likely lead to its spiritual growth.

Be grateful to all existences that have a soul and are accomplishing their mission

What, then, should people do for plants? First, we must understand that plants have emotions and that they have souls. This is the starting point of everything. When we realize that plants are giving their life to create the environment we live in, we develop a heart of gratitude toward all things. We feel grateful toward both plants and animals, as well as other things in nature, like land, mountains, and rocks. Humans assume these things do not have consciousness, but they do. In fact, even minerals have souls. Although their souls change very slowly, there is no doubt that they have souls.

Even a diamond, for instance, has a soul. There needs to be a soul dwelling in a diamond to create the kind of crystal they have. The soul of a diamond spiritually influences the person wearing it. You can see this visibly. When women wear diamonds, they clearly look different. This is because diamonds are affecting them in reality. Within a diamond there is a life force; it is not just a simple glass marble. Although the life of a diamond is slow and motionless, it is accomplishing its mission, slowly but steadily.

Likewise, gems and ores are not born by coincidence. They are not made by chance but are created because they have a mission.

This is why it is important to give gratitude to everything on this earth that you can see with your eyes.

3

The Secret behind the Souls of Animals, Plants, and Minerals

Q3

You have said that people's thoughts influence their environment; you also mentioned that animals, plants, and minerals have souls. Then, how do people's thoughts influence animals, plants, and minerals? If they are in places filled with very good thoughts or vibrations, I presume there will be no problems. But what if they are in places with bad vibrations? For example, some plants are growing in war zones; there are also roadside trees and bonsai trees; some trees are planted in hospitals. Do they all grow in different places like this for the purpose of soul training?

The Ninth Public Lecture of 1989, "What Is the Ultimate of Enlightenment?"
Held on December 17, 1989 at Ryogoku Kokugikan Sumo Arena in Tokyo, Japan

Plants may have a more refined vibration than humans do

There are floral wreaths on a stand in front of me and below them are pots of red flowers, or red leaves to be precise. They are popular around this time of the year—the Christmas season. We have this flower at home as well, but since I was away for a few days and couldn't water it, I found it withered when I returned home. Seeing this, I thought, "Oh no, it's all withered. Poor thing." So I used my hand power and gave it light saying, "Please bloom once more. Restore your old self." Then, the next day, it had restored its original state. It was fully blooming and seemed very energetic. Usually, a withered flower will not come back to life, but my flower was brimming with energy. This happened after I spoke to it.

In this way, plants feel and respond to what humans say. They react to subtle things, so their souls must have a very refined vibration. Perhaps plant souls have more refined vibrations than humans do. This may be because, unlike humans, plants are always in a meditative state, so they are more sensitive to vibrations.

The relationship between music and plant growth is being researched in agricultural chemistry, and it seems they are making great progress. Out of all the music genres, the waltz seems to make plants bear more fruit and grow the fastest. Plants grow very fast when a waltz is played but wither when it is rock music. However, if they listen to waltz music all day long, they forget to grow. So for plants to grow fast, it is best that you play waltz music for them just before daybreak. If plant souls listen to music when the sunlight is emerging at the start of the day, they get excited and think, "I must make efforts to grow today." This causes them to grow rapidly. I have heard about this.

All plants have souls that respond in ways like this and the same goes for animals.

Even animal spirits go to either heaven or hell after death

We, humans, tend to describe animals as instinctive. We often say that animals have instincts whereas humans have minds, but it is not as simple as that. Animals also have basic emotions like humans. They feel joy, anger, sadness, and pleasure. Like humans, animals live under the principle of self-responsibility, so they are responsible for what they feel. If that wasn't the case, why do some animal spirits fall to hell? If they were simply living according to what their instincts tell them, no judgment would be made of them. However, animal spirits go to either heaven or hell after death. They are held accountable for the feelings they choose to have toward things while they are alive. This is a fundamental principle. What is expected from animals is not as complicated as what is expected of humans, but they will be tested on how they live based on their feelings of joy, anger, sadness, or pleasure, and whether they choose to create suffering or happiness. This is what is expected of animals.

Humans and animals such as domesticated animals, are living very closely in this world. Their happiness and unhappiness are easily affected by the humans they live with. As proof of this, we often see pets take after their owners, which is a widely known phenomenon. Pets will have different temperaments depending on the kind of words their owners speak to them every day. This is true. If the owner is always irritated and agitated and takes his anger out on his surroundings, his pet will do the same. It will also feel the need to take its anger out on something. Pets in these situations are constantly irritated and, in the case of dogs, they tend to bark a lot.

In this way, the various vibrations that people emit affect animals and plants.

What do plants and animals think of the current age?

There are two types of effects the vibrations of humans have on plants and animals. One is the effect they have on individual souls, which I just mentioned. The second is the effect they have on an entire group of souls.

Plants and animals living in the current age indeed feel that they are in an age of crisis. This is because they cannot protect themselves by their own means. In more peaceful times, they were able to do things to protect their species. But now, in this age, humans are changing the environment drastically, and because of that, the environment for plants and animals is also changing. For example, humans are depriving plants of their living environment, which is an obvious fact. The same goes for animals. For instance, cats don't even catch mice anymore. I haven't analyzed how this will affect the souls of cats, but I believe it was the cats' job to catch mice in return for food. Given they don't anymore, we can say that this will probably have a significant impact on the soul training of cats.

The current age has a lot of negative effects on animals in terms of their environment. But if you look at it positively, now is actually a chance for animals to acquire human-like emotions. This is because we are living in an age where humans and animals are living very closely. It is a chance for animals to learn more about human emotions. The souls of domesticated animals are actually more advanced compared to other animal souls. Souls that have lived as domesticated animals for many lifetimes are able to understand the human mind to quite a high level.

How do animal souls evolve into human souls?

Unlike the process of evolution set out in the phylogenetic tree, most creatures were intended to be created as they are. Humans were created as humans and animals as animals. The concept of "what you are" is engraved in your soul to an extent. But since the entire universe is in the process of evolution, souls can change this original concept and transform into something different. Although it is very rare, sometimes an animal soul will evolve into a human soul.

What are the conditions for an animal soul to evolve into a human soul? One is that they have been born as domesticated animals several times, lived closely with humans, and can understand the basic lifestyle and emotions of humans. Another condition is that they have lived an exceptional life that is worthy of receiving the "highest achievement award" within the animal species. To give you an example, it would be to live like the dog Lassie. Another example would be living as a guide dog. Some guide dogs have very high-level souls. If you look at some human beings, they couldn't care less about others; they neglect people in need. On the contrary, despite being animals, guide dogs help people in need by becoming their hands and feet. The souls of dogs who live a life like this will make considerable spiritual growth. They are practicing giving love and aiding humans in their daily lives.

Of course, these dogs have to go through training, but once they reach a certain level, they are permitted to be born as a human. This training is given by various gods who reside in the sixth dimensional realm and guide animals. They are known as Inari Daimyojin* in Japan. This is how animals can become humans.

When animals are born as humans, some will succeed greatly, but many actually fail at living as humans. This is because they are not used to the human lifestyle after all. Some of them behave unbelievably in the eyes of ordinary human beings. Please do not take this the wrong way or misunderstand me, but some people do things that a person with basic human emotions would never think of doing. For example, they could have a desire to steal something just because it is there. Some people feel the urge to steal things even though this should not be allowed on an ethical level.

Others may be very aggressive or quick-tempered though this is quite common among humans. In any case, some people show extreme reactions and animal-like traits.

In this way, when some animal souls fail to live as humans, they are reverted to their original form. They will be made to learn once again how wonderful it is to be born as a human.

Some animal spirits can speak human words

This is something I must say because it is the truth, so I will be blunt: some souls that dwell in animals were human in the past. I wish this were not true, but in some exceptional cases, human souls reside in animal bodies. In the world beyond this one called hell, there is the infamous Hell of Beasts, which has been known since long ago. This hell is a world of animals. People who fall into this hell turn into animals. Their souls take on the form of a particular animal that is closest to their mindset.

Someone with a habit of lying will appear as an animal that most symbolizes a liar, such as a fox. A person who tends to be jealous or spiteful of people will turn into a snake. As you can see from these examples, people whose minds possess the trait of a particular animal for a long time will transform into that animal. This is because the other world is a world of thoughts. There are no material things or physical matter there. Because it is a world of thoughts, people will change into exactly what their minds are like.

Many souls who live in this kind of hell for a long time forget that they are actually human and instead think that they are animal souls, such as snakes or foxes. They start to possess living people and cause them trouble. So when I talk to animal spirits that possess humans, many of them speak human languages. Purely animal souls cannot speak much. They only have basic emotions and can only answer "yes" or "no." However, you will find that some animal souls speak very well. That is because they are actually human souls. They were originally human but ended up becoming animals. Most of these souls believe that they are animals, although some are aware that they are not.

People who fall into this hell may stay there for several hundred or a thousand years, and in some cases, much longer than that. As they spend a long time there, they forget about their human form and the fact that they are human. But even in a world like that, it is still possible for them to eventually attain enlightenment, although it won't be of a high level. When they grow sick of being in the Hell of Beasts and start repenting for their actions, they can sometimes attain an above-average level of enlightenment.

When these spirits are permitted to be born again, it is very rare for them to be born as humans straightaway. In most cases, they are first born as the animals of which they took the shape when they were in hell. You will find these kinds of souls among the domesticated animals. Some animals understand human emotions so well that they creep you out. They are so perceptive of emotions that you would think that they are human. Among these animals, some actually used to be humans.

These souls undergo such harsh spiritual training. If you imagine what they have to go through, you will understand that it truly is severe training. The toughest part about it is that they aren't able to communicate their thoughts. These souls can understand words and what humans are saying. They can understand what humans are conversing or feeling, but they cannot express their own thoughts through words. This is a very painful discipline, but through it, these souls will realize how difficult and how much of a blessing it is to be born as a human. After realizing this, they can return to their original path of evolution and go back to being a human.

As you can see, there are times when souls regress in the process of evolution, but if you look at it from a long-term perspective, they are evolving overall. We can say that.

Plants exist in the spiritual world

Now, let me talk more about plant souls. It is very difficult for a human soul to dwell in a plant. Humans and plants have different modes of existence, so a soul who has been living as a human for a long time will find it difficult to be born as a plant.

That being said, some plants have a mental structure similar to that of humans. Some souls of trees and flowers are at a very high spiritual level. As you can imagine, this is particularly the case for plants that have lived for several hundred or over a thousand years. When you observe them using spiritual sight, you can see that their souls look similar to human souls. Some people say that fairies exist in trees, flowers, and other things, and they are right. Fairies are actually the souls of nature.

The level of enlightenment of those plants is definitely not low. That is why plants exist in the Spirit World, namely the fourth dimensional Astral Realm, the fifth dimensional Goodness Realm, the sixth dimensional Light Realm, and the seventh dimensional Bodhisattva Realm. Plants in these worlds exist as a manifestation of their souls so they do not look like the plants in this world. The fact that these souls appear in a particular dimension in heaven means that they are souls of that level or dimension.

Whether it be animals or plants, their leader souls are very spiritually advanced. These leaders make vows to God and take on a leading role. For example, the leader of flowers will lead the entire flower group, and likewise for trees. So these souls are at a very high spiritual level. When explained in terms of human souls, some plants have attained an enlightenment close to that of a bodhisattva. These plant souls have deeper emotions than those of humans. They dwell in plants when they are living on earth, and for a very long time, they stand still and observe the world around them and how it changes as time goes by. They live with such things in mind.

Minerals have souls and are going through very slow soul training during their long lives

Therefore, please do not think that only humans can think or that only humans have souls. On this earth, all things have souls. The difference is the speed at which they live. Animals move, but plants move less. Minerals rarely move. Souls of minerals have a longer lifespan than plants; they live over a much longer time frame. We, humans, will come to the end of our lives in 60 or 70 years, but minerals live for a very, very long time. They have a lifespan of tens of thousands, hundreds of thousands, or millions of years. They spend this much time developing their souls.

For example, a diamond is made from carbon. Carbon lies deep below the earth's surface and, as it is subjected to heat and pressure, it becomes a diamond. This is the birth of a life form. The necessary components bond together and a gem is born. After being born, it will remain underground for the next two or three million years until it comes to the surface during a volcanic eruption. It will then be unearthed by people who dig for diamonds in areas like South Africa and used in rings, necklaces, and some other things. Eventually, it will be thrown away or buried somewhere and its molecular structure will break down.

Minerals live very long lives, during which they go through a process of birth, growth, and death. What is different about them is the length of their lifespan. In this way, some living things go through a very slow evolution process and they, too, have souls. I can say this because the very same minerals that exist in this world exist in the other world, too. There is iron, gold, silver, and copper in the other world. There are also diamonds, rubies, sapphires, and other gems. They all exist in the other world, which means they all have souls. These souls also come down to earth to undergo training in a physical form.

Some may laugh at me for saying this, but the lives of minerals are on a completely different timescale to that of humans, where one second for them could be equal to ten thousand years for us. Some things are undergoing this kind of slow soul training. In this way, various life forms are living together in the same time period. I would like people to understand this and realize that all living things are affecting each other as they live.

[Editor's note]
Inari Daimyojin is essentially a position title for high spirits who specialize in guiding animal spirits. They reside in the upper level of the sixth dimensional Light Realm. Unfortunately, the current Inari worship in Japan has become a means to satisfy worldly desires such as praying for business success. It is no longer a kind of faith to worship the gods who are in charge of protecting animals. At the Inari shrines, lost animal spirits gather as they are drawn to the earthly desires of the people who visit, and sometimes bring them misfortune. At times, even human souls that have fallen to the Hell of Beasts disguise themselves as the Inari Daimyojin and lead people astray. (Refer to *An Unshakable Mind* [New York: IRH Press, 2023])

4

What Happens to Human Souls after Death?

Q4

We are taught that the essence of a human is the spirit. But we are also taught that when humans die and shed their physical bodies, their astral bodies remain, and after casting off their astral bodies, their spirit bodies remain, and underneath those are light bodies, and so on. We are taught that humans will always have these bodies or vessels. However, if their true essence is God's Light that dwells in them, not the vessels that are cast off, it would ultimately mean that only God, Himself, is the essence of humans, so there is no essence to individual humans. On another occasion, you have taught us that our essence is the mind, which has an onion-like structure.

After hearing all of this, it sounds like we do not have just one mind but two or three differently shaped minds. Could you please tell us how we should understand the spiritual essence of a human?

The First Lecture of the Lecture Series for Kansai Branch,
"Utopia and Utopian Values"
Held on May 12, 1989 at Osaka Cultural Hall for Small- and
Mid-Sized Businesses in Osaka, Japan

The human spirit is made up of multiple entities

Listening to your question, I get a sense that your understanding of "form" and "idea" is mixed up. That is because your view is based on this third dimensional world, which is not the correct way to think; it should be the other way around. The right way to look at the world is that everything started from an idea, which then took form. You, on the other hand, are looking at the world based on the physical body and working backward. That is incorrect.

First, let's think about the essence of an astral body. A human being is indeed a single spirit body, but to be more accurate, we are a complex body of multiple life forms. All of our organs, such as our heart and lungs, have their own consciousness. So, despite being small, each of them is a single life form. Moreover, every single cell in our body is alive. Cells are small but each one has a soul and a small, dot-like mind that allows them to live. We are a collective body of these small life forms.

Then, what will happen when I die? My physical body will be cremated, but I will live on as a collective body of consciousnesses. These consciousnesses are what make up the fourth dimensional astral body. So, although my physical body will be gone, my appearance won't change because my astral body maintains it. The astral body contains all of the souls of the organs, so it preserves the person's physical appearance.

This is how human spirits look shortly after returning from the third dimensional world. But, as they continue to live in their astral body in the Astral Realm for a long time, many of the components that make up the astral body become unnecessary. The cells, the heart, and the lungs no longer need to function, so their consciousnesses start to get fuzzy or unclear. Next, these consciousnesses enter a hibernation-like state and lose their shape. Eventually, they turn into a thin film that sticks to the core of the soul and gradually becomes inactive. They become like a thin mochi layer of *Yukimi Daifuku* (mochi ice cream). There will no longer be individual life forms such as a heart, lung, or kidney. At this point, the soul is ready to cast off the astral body because it is no longer necessary. And that is what it will do.

At first, astral bodies that have been cast off are soft and they float about. They can sometimes appear like ghosts if they are floating near the earthly world. This soft astral body gradually loses its form and will be dispersed and turned into various types of energy. These energies are generally used to create scenery and landscapes in the fourth dimensional world. They become the elements for various things that are to be expressed there, such as flowers blooming, houses being built, and living creatures. This is one way that astral bodies are used.

Cast-off astral bodies can also be reused when an old soul is reborn on earth. Very old souls cannot recall the senses of the physical body because it's been so long since they last dwelled in one. So they cannot make their own astral body. In that situation, the astral body of a soul that recently lived on earth will be used. The old soul will wear it and be reborn into this world. Because cast-off astral bodies are used for this purpose, they are stored as outer garments in the Astral Realm.

What does it mean to evolve spiritually?

This is the situation in the Astral Realm. When you go to higher dimensions, you will become less concerned about shape and form, and your sense of the physical body will fade. You will go from a world *with* form to a world *without* form.

In other words, your true soul does not have a form. At least by the time spirits reach the upper level of the sixth dimensional world, they know that their true form is not that of a human. At this point, they can transform their body in any way they like. This is how the spirits there become.

If a spirit still has a strong sense of being human, it will feel uncomfortable not having a form. If you have a strong sense of being human in the other world, it means your level of enlightenment is still low. You will be told by other spirits, "Don't talk like a human." [*Audience laughs.*] It sounds funny but you will be told, "Stop sounding like a living human being." Basically, they are calling you stupid for thinking from a physical perspective. In fact, spirits in even higher dimensions find it embarrassing that they had to take on a physical form. They think it is embarrassing that they had hands, feet, and mouths, and that they even had to eat. This is because they exist as thoughts. You (the questioner) may feel that you cannot exist without taking on a physical form, but the high spirits exist as thoughts.

For instance, in the Spirit World, you may be told to become a jellyfish and float to train your consciousness. If you feel uncomfortable not having a human form, you won't be able to do this. On the contrary, a high spirit exists as a body of consciousness and does not recognize itself as a visible form with hands and feet. Instead, it simply recognizes itself as the work it does under a ray of Buddha's light, such as the white light, red light, or some other color (as taught in Happy Science). When it's necessary to show itself to people, it takes on a particular form. A high spirit can appear in a particular form when it meets other spirits or guides people on earth, but that is not its true form.

For example, a high spirit under the light of politics acts as a thought that guides politics, and a high spirit under the light of the medical field acts as a thought in that field. When you see such a high spirit, it really looks like a ray of light. When it is resting, it is a mass of light, and when it begins to work, it turns into a ray of light. It shines ever so brilliantly. This is how high spirits work.

I, too, will return to the Spirit World in several decades. Perhaps I will meet you, but at that time, I will not have eyes, a nose, or a mouth. Even so, please recognize me. This is how things will be.

It may be very difficult for you to understand this idea as it is contrary to how people think in the third dimensional world. When you start to understand this idea, it means you are evolving spiritually. We have published books that talk about abstract matters like this such as *Spiritual Messages from Socrates* (now republished as *A Collection of Spiritual Messages by Ryuho Okawa Vol. 9* in Japanese, only available at Happy Science temples and branches), so please read them carefully and try to understand them. If you can understand the ideas introduced in these books, it means you have advanced a lot in your spiritual level.

CHAPTER TWO

The Earthly World, the Spirit World, and Hell

1

Right View in a World of Abundance

Q1

Now, in this world of abundance, material objects are easily being thrown away and being handled without much regard in households. When I see objects being treated that way, I feel sorry for them. My question is, do material objects have a negative impact on people's lives?

Intermediate Level Seminar in 1988
Held on June 12, 1988 at Sabo Hall in Tokyo, Japan

Why do religions often deny material objects?

OK. Many religions tend to first teach people to deny material objects. In Buddhism, too, the teachings start with denying material objects and worldly matters. This is always the first stage in religion. For a religion to teach people that humans are essentially beings of the mind or spirit, it must first deny material objects and the physical body. Otherwise, people will not awaken to their spirituality so easily. So, the first step in teaching religious truth is to deny material objects, which will bring a 180-degree shift in people's way of thinking. This is a necessary step.

People will not be able to receive religious teachings if they think, "This is my body. This is me, this is what I am." That is why religions teach, "The physical self is not the real self" as the foundational teaching. After that, they go on to teach that humans are essentially the spirit or the soul. Then, people will begin to accept these teachings.

As people continue to live their lives, they will come across the issue of "how to view physical objects." So, the next step is to teach them that physical objects are materials used to polish one's soul. When people are taught this, they experience another 180-degree shift in their view, so in the end, they go through a 360-degree shift. This means people's worldview will return to where it started and they will see material objects as something important. When their worldview changes, people will recognize the importance of material objects, except this time, the word "important" takes on a different meaning. When people gain the perspective that all things in this world are there to help them in their soul training, they see material items in a completely different light. For example, if they took care of their material possessions from a moral perspective before, they will now do so from a different perspective.

Humans are simple-minded creatures, so we will not understand religious teachings unless we first deny the material world. Humans must be taught step-by-step. After denying the material world, they can then move on to think about the truth behind how God created this world. Only then will they deeply appreciate material objects and the convenience of this world.

I truly feel this sense of gratitude towards the material world when I converse with the spirit of a certain religious leader who has recently left this world. I have been publishing many of his spiritual messages. When he was still alive, he repeatedly taught that humans are not physical bodies. But after leaving this world, he said, "Although I was short and scrawny, I was able to talk in front of everyone because I had a physical body. I was able to teach the Laws and see the face of each person because I had a body. This was a truly invaluable and cherishable experience."

Many of you probably have all kinds of inferiority complex about your body. But the aforementioned spirit told me, "Although I had a frail body, I was able to tell others about myself, share my thoughts, respond to their reactions in various ways, talk with them, and convey the Truth. These were all happy things."

Once you become a spirit, you will no longer be able to talk directly to living humans even if you have attained a high level of enlightenment and are in the world of Light. Considering this, the spirit of the religious leader I mentioned reminisced over how precious it was to have a physical body. But this does not mean he is attached to it. Rather, he saw the physical body and material objects as God's Grace.

Discover greater love by gaining the true worldview

We often say that the modern age is a materialistic civilization, however, within this exists something of importance. As mentioned in *The Spiritual Teachings by Edison* (only available in Japanese), we are able to undergo soul training at a very fast pace and with great intensity, thanks to the convenience and benefits the materialistic civilization has provided us with.

Let me give you an example. To attend the seminar today, some of you from Osaka may have come via the bullet train this morning while others may have flown in by airplane last night. But regardless of the type of transportation you used, you were able to get here because the age we live in allowed you that option. If it was 100 years ago or even further back, it would have been impossible for you to make that choice. So, we should be grateful that we can now easily travel from one place to another, and we should not say that physical objects are not good for us and reject them entirely. You must know that there is a valuable aspect to them.

Therefore, first, you need to awaken to spirituality by denying objects completely. Then, the next step is to realize that this material world, or the three dimensional world, is actually a marvelous world of God's self-expression or God's art; it is to learn that there is a meaning to every existence and that this world is given as a training ground for all beings to train their souls. You should feel this first-hand and awaken to this Truth. If you do not, it means you have wasted your life. Please think like that.

As people attain higher enlightenment, they will realize how important physical objects are in the truest sense. Even the microphone that I am speaking into now is something to be grateful for. If I did not have it, I would have to shout at the top of my lungs. So, it is something to be thankful for. I want to say, "Thank you, Mr. Microphone." In this way, people should become more grateful even for the little things as they attain higher enlightenment.

None of you here probably know this, but there is a fan underneath this podium that has been blowing air on me. I did not realize this at the beginning of today's lecture, but after a while, I felt a breeze around my legs and saw that a fan had been placed there. Someone in charge of setting up the podium had kindly put the fan there. How thoughtful of them. Indeed, there are many things to appreciate in this world. I should also say, "Thank you, Mr. Fan."

In this way, denying the material objects does not mean you should deny their existence entirely. In fact, you will develop deeper gratitude toward the little things when you discover how many blessings surround you. Once you do, you will find that all living things in this world are shining brightly and you will be able to see the world in a completely different light.

In the old days, Shakyamuni Buddha awakened to this perspective. He saw that the mountains, rivers, grass, trees, and land all have Buddha-nature and that they are manifestations of the Primordial Buddha's energy. What he did was that he first refuted the physical body and material existences as false and entered the world of the soul. But he then refuted that too, and saw how wonderful this world was. When you look at everything in the world through this new perspective, they all appear wonderful. This is how your worldview will change.

Some of you may attend a Happy Science seminar, take a test, and be ranked according to your test scores, which may be frustrating, but you need to be grateful for the fact that other people exist. Because they exist, we are encouraged and motivated to do better and work hard together. If we were alone, we would be clueless as to where we stand. Because there are excellent people and—I don't know how to phrase this but—not-so-excellent people, our souls can be polished. This is something we should be grateful for. Indeed, you will become grateful for everything.

To gain this perspective is the same as discovering greater love. This greater love will then turn into energy for you to do missionary work. This is what I believe.

2

The Power of Light That Is Creating This World

Q2

Happy Science teaches a whole new worldview that has never been taught before. In the past, people came up with various types of beliefs, such as materialism and *Yui-shin-ron* [a belief that the mind is the fundamental reality], but I think we can summarize and say that Happy Science explains the world theoretically in terms of light. So, I would like you to teach us about the power and the workings of light.

The Fifth Grand Lecture of 1990, Part II "Speaking on the Royal Road of Life"
Held on June 3, 1990 at Makuhari Messe in Chiba, Japan

All things are created from attributes of light

OK, I will teach you.

There are various explanations about the world and they are named differently. At Happy Science, as you have accurately described, we start by explaining what light is. This explanation is very much unique to Happy Science.

For example, one of the other religious groups explains that the physical body and material objects are not real and that only the other world is real. This idea is a little different from what we teach at Happy Science. Of course, we also teach that the world we go to after death is the Real World, but if we trace back to the absolute origin of the Real World, we end up at God's Light, which is the source of all light. As God's Light comes down to the lower dimensions, various realms of the Spirit World are created along the way. It gradually comes down and creates the third dimension, which is the material world. So, the components that make up the objects of the material world are none other than spiritual existences. This is the reality. An object is made up of small particles of light that make up spiritual matter. When these particles of light reach the Phenomenal World, they solidify and come together to form objects. This is our theory.

Other religious groups are trying to provide a theoretical explanation for this through physical phenomena, but at Happy Science, we do not take that approach. Some groups are conducting experiments to make an object go through a wall. They have been trying to make an object go through another, which has recently become a hot topic. These experiments are proving that what we believe as material objects can actually dissipate into a gas state and also return to their original form. In fact, they all start with something that looks like a small dot called a spiriton, and when it gets charged, we call it a photon. A photon is actually the smallest unit of matter that makes up an object. The truth is that photons gather to form atoms, which then form molecules. This is our theory.

So, just as you (the questioner) think, we believe in the monism of *light as the source of everything*. In other words, we believe in the idea that all things are created from the attributes of light. There are many different ways to explain how this world works. For instance, people can differentiate this world from the other world or distinguish objects and the physical body from the spirit. Nevertheless, these explanations serve as expedients to make it easier for people to understand.

Some people may find it easier to understand if you explain that this world and the other world are two separate worlds. You can explain to them, "The other world is the real world and this world is a temporary world" or "This world is a mirage-like world that does not really exist." This is not wrong. However, you must know that they are explanations to simplify the idea so that people will be able to understand. The truth is that, as we have been saying, God's Light manifests in various ways and all worlds of the third dimension and higher were created by God.

3

How Was the Spirit World Created?

Q3

In *The Laws of the Sun* (New York: IRH Press, 2018), there are two explanations for how the Spirit World was created: one says that it began with creating the higher dimensions, while the other says that the lower-level Spirit World came first. Could you please clarify this?

The First Seminar for Regional Managers in 1994,
"Q&A Session on *The Laws of the Sun*"
Held on July 26, 1994 at Hotel Kajima no Mori in Nagano, Japan

How the dimensional structure was built on Earth

It is difficult to explain dimensions. When you build a ten-story building, you cannot build the second floor and then build the tenth floor. That is not how buildings are made—we must build floor by floor.

As for the Spirit World, however, it was created through a different process. [*While drawing on the whiteboard*] This is Earth—or Gaia, as how some people refer to it recently—and the Earth Consciousness dwells in it. It emits vibrations, or an aura, as a living being. The Earth gives off a great amount of this aura. This was how it was originally. The Earth itself is a life form, so it gives off an aura and creates a field of energy.

Next, when a spirit of a higher dimension added purpose to this field of energy, the will to create a spiritual field began to be carried out. This is similar to how iron sand forms many layers of curved lines around a bar magnet—I am sure you have done this kind of experiment before when you were a student. Anyhow, when a higher dimensional spirit gave purpose to this field of energy, rings formed in the spiritual field around the Earth like a ripple, similar to how iron filings smoothly line up in a magnetic field. This was how dimensions were created.

In the beginning, the Earth's Spirit World was merely an ambiguous field of energy surrounding the Earth. But as the will to create a spiritual field worked on Earth and things settled, multiple layers of the spiritual field were formed. This is the dimensional structure of the Earth's Spirit World.

Master Ryuho Okawa explained how the Earth's dimensional structure was created while drawing on the whiteboard.

How the living space for spirits in the other world was created

After that came the issue of what to put inside the Spirit World. A place for spirits to live had to be made inside the spiritual field and this required a lot of effort. So, it was thanks to the power of various spirits that many realms were established in the other world. They have made many things.

In the beginning, there were only spiritual fields, but now, there are mountains, valleys, and rivers in the other world. These things certainly did not appear all of a sudden. They appeared because the consciousness of spirits who were born on earth and had returned to the other world sought such landscapes. This is because when they were alive, they lived in places surrounded by rivers and mountains. In the other world, when a group of spirits with a similar consciousness gather and form collective thoughts such as, "There should be mountains here and rivers over there," those sceneries appear. In this way, when spirits form a collective thought, a concrete and appropriate training ground gradually forms in the other world.

Let me illustrate an example. In the rear side of the Spirit World, spirits who like to undergo discipline all favor a rocky terrain. When they were alive, they may have been *yamabushi* (mountain monks) who underwent training by climbing mountains and such. Since they trained in a rocky environment, they strongly seek a place like that in the other world, too. Consequently, a world expressed through these thoughts will form in the Spirit World, and spirits who wish to live in such an environment will gather.

It has taken over tens or hundreds of millions of years to make various living spaces in the other world. They have been created and developed by the collective thoughts of the spirits. Currently, reinforced concrete buildings are standing in the fourth and fifth dimensions of the other world. People who lived in these kinds of houses while they were alive retain their consciousnesses of having lived in them, so they naturally want to live in such houses in the other world, too. As more spirits with a similar consciousness return to the Spirit World, the more reinforced concrete houses there will be. Upon seeing the change, other spirits will be embarrassed for not keeping up with the latest trend, so they will start recreating their houses. In this way, innovation is also occurring in the other world.

The Genesis of the Spirit World is a highly advanced teaching that is part of the Laws of El Cantare

In the beginning, the Earth only had an aura and within it, small microorganisms lived and died. As they continued to do that, an ambiguous lower-level Spirit World formed around the surface of the Earth. This is the truth. Afterward, with the power of the tenth dimensional and ninth dimensional spirits, different dimensions were created in a way similar to how magnetic fields work around a magnet. With the energies of the Earth Consciousness and other high spirits, the Spirit World was magnetized and split into multiple dimensions. Just as how light splits into several colors when it passes through a prism, multiple dimensions were formed.

If God were to get rid of these dimensions, He could do so just by shrinking everything in an instant. That will restore Earth to how it was when it was first created. When the soul training on Earth comes to an end, everything will revert to its original state. The entire dimensional structure will be undone in an instant. If God decides that it is no longer necessary for living beings to train on Earth, everything will return to its original state, and eventually, Earth itself will vanish. That is when it dies, in other words, when the Earth becomes a black hole. This will come in approximately five billion years.

This is how things work. The Spirit World is actually quite similar to the world of electromagnetic waves. Dimensions are, in other words, fields of energy. So, energy fields were first created, and then with the thoughts of many spirits, various living spaces were created within them. Therefore, to answer your question about whether the ninth dimension was created first or the lower-level Spirit World existed first, I would say yes to both. At first, there was indeed a lower-level Spirit World where microorganisms lived, but it was still not fully established. The Spirit World was then split into different dimensional levels. Then, as advanced life forms repeated their cycle of reincarnation, hell became fully established, and as for the heavenly world, the dimensions became more distinct.

What I would like to say is that there is certainly the Genesis of the Spirit World. The principle of creation is part of the Laws of El Cantare. This is a highly advanced teaching. Perhaps I will teach about this later on, but there is no need for me to teach it now.

There are more details on the "updated version" of the Genesis, but I do not think now is the time to talk about it. I don't believe we have to be in such a hurry to know this. Please think like that.

4

The Difference between Evil Spirits in the Abysmal Hell and Satans

Q4

Among the spirits who have fallen into the Abysmal Hell, some are going through excruciating pain in the Hell of Agonizing Cries or the Great Hell of Agonizing Cries, while others are wreaking havoc as satans (devils) in hell. What is the difference between them?

The First Seminar for Regional Managers in 1994,
"Q&A Session on *The Laws of the Sun*"
Held on July 26, 1994 at Hotel Kajima no Mori in Nagano, Japan

What turns a spirit into a satan are long years in hell and strong willpower

One thing that makes evil spirits and satans different from each other is the number of years spent in hell. It takes a good amount of years for a spirit to become a satan. Imagine prison gang leaders—the longer they are in prison, the more powerful they become. The same applies to the spirits in hell; they are quite clueless when they first fall to hell, but as hundreds, one thousand, or two thousand years go by, they become old-timers and recruit their own henchmen. Newcomers keep coming to hell, so old-timers will use them as their subordinates or underlings. By doing so, these old-timer spirits slowly establish their positions as satans. What is more, they cannot be reborn, so they have been in hell for a very long time.

Another difference is willpower, which is also a form of spiritual power. Some spirits in hell have extremely strong willpower. This might have to do with the work they have accumulated throughout their past lives. You see, when a person in a high position commits destruction, it influences many people. These include high-ranking but ill-natured military officers and politicians, corrupt prime ministers, and malicious small-company presidents. In any case, when such people commit evil, the destruction they cause is considerable.

People who caused large-scale destruction while they were alive have very strong willpower, which is effective in the other world, too. Spirits with strong willpower can control other spirits with weaker willpower. They have accumulated their strong willpower over the course of their past lives.

You can also think of devils as spirits who were given more or less an important role from heaven in their lives but went astray. Think of it as a promotion in a bad sense. This can happen. People often say, "A very good person can turn into a very evil person," and the opposite can also happen. In other words, once a very good and competent person turns evil, they can become a great devil. Likewise, a powerful devil who repents deeply and cooperates with good people might do excellent work. These things can happen.

In a sense, people's "work skills" are something they have developed over many, many years of reincarnation, and each person has their own level of capability.

5
Why Did Darwin Fall to Hell?

Q5

In *The Golden Laws* (Tokyo: HS Press, 2015), you mentioned that Darwin was not a hypocritical person, but because he taught a materialistic philosophy, he fell into the Abysmal Hell and is going through self-reflection. What does this mean?

The First Seminar to Appoint New Associate Lecturers,
"A Lecture on *How to Exorcise Evil Spirits*"
Held on February 11, 1990 at Nippon Seinenkan in Tokyo, Japan

---

The dangers of spreading harmful thinking by teaching a mistaken philosophy

This goes for religion, too, but teaching a philosophy comes at a very high risk. When people return to the other world, they are usually judged based on whether their thoughts and actions while they were alive were good or evil. But this judgment will work differently for religious leaders and philosophers since their power of influence is not of the average person and they have great influence.

Please think about a movie film as an example. A drop of ink on a film does not look too dirty when it is not in use, but when you put it under a light to show an image or a movie, you will see a big stain. Likewise, when someone with a great power of influence makes mistakes, it leads to dire consequences. Generally, when people make mistakes, they will be forgiven if they repent, but this is not the case for people with a larger sphere of influence. Mistakes that these people make will affect a much larger number of people. If the thoughts they spread bring serious harm to people's minds, it would be very difficult to undo the damage. The consequences of conveying wrong thoughts are dire. For this reason, religious leaders and philosophers have great responsibility.

Let me give you an example of the consequences of establishing the wrong philosophy. Several years ago, a book titled *The Closing of the American Mind* became a best-seller in the U.S.A. It was translated into Japanese as well and published by Misuzu Shobo. I was reading this book and thought that it was saying good things, but a problem occurred when I got to the section where the author commented on Nietzsche. There is a part in the book in which the author highly praises Nietzsche and his philosophy. To clarify, I was reading a Japanese translation, so of course, it was translated by a Japanese person. The author of the original book was also a different thinker, not Nietzsche himself, and he was simply explaining Nietzsche's philosophy. Despite this, when I reached the part about Nietzsche, I felt very sick and began to get dizzy. However, as soon as I got past that part, I felt better. The rest of the book was well-written. I only felt sick when I read that particular section. It was a very strange experience.

My point is that establishing a philosophy comes at a very high risk. Even if another person explains it, a wrong philosophy will continue to emit a negative influence and affect people. Establishing a thought means you will leave this much of a powerful influence, so it is a very risky thing to do.

This is especially true with Marxism. I'm sure there are pure-hearted people among those who support Marxism, but you must observe what happens to those who lead others by confidently upholding this philosophy. For example, Marxism influenced Japan as well, and this movement began with labor union activities, which led to many other things. Interestingly, when companies begin to incorporate labor unions, they face financial difficulties. It is as if these companies are targeted by evil spirits and their situations keep getting worse. A good example of this is the Japanese National Railways (now known as the Japan Railways Group). Companies that incorporate labor unions often face problems as though they are taken over by evil spirits. They face difficulties, create many evils, and take from those around them.

In the field of education, there are activities held by the Japan Teachers' Union. When you look at each member individually, they might be a very kind father to their family or a teacher with extensive knowledge. I'm sure many of them are like that on a personal level. However, the philosophy behind their activities will clearly be deemed wrong in the eyes of God. So if they are spreading wrong ideas through their activities, it will no longer be a mistake on an individual level. If wrong ideas are spread on a large scale, they cannot be taken back; that is how much influence they have on others. Therefore, people who are active in the Japan Teachers' Union need to think about the negative effect they will have on children that comes with teaching the wrong thoughts or philosophies. These wrongdoings cannot be amended through individual self-reflection. Please be aware of that.

There are, however, some cases when union activities are serving justice, for instance, when they are fighting against the poverty of the entire society. In such situations, their activities are overlooked to an extent and they are forgiven. But their actions become evil in cases when they are not appropriate.

How can Darwin and Marx be saved?

Here is the sad part. Regarding Marxism, for example, Marx himself was not an evil person. He used to be an angel. However, what has become of his philosophy? What has become of China? What has become of the Soviet Union? The answers to these questions are obvious if you look at the several decades of history and ask whether his philosophy stood the test of time. What was the result of Marxism? It created a kind of hell. This shows that his philosophy was wrong. So, the one who gave birth to this philosophy must take responsibility. That is why his sin would only be forgiven when the Soviet Union (at the time of the lecture), China, and North Korea collapse and establish new regimes and when people stop condemning Marx. Until then, he will continue to suffer in hell. This is how grave of a mistake it is to establish wrong ideas.

Establishing a philosophy comes with a very high risk. If you were to build a nation under the wrong philosophy, it would affect hundreds of millions of people for dozens of years. How will you take responsibility for that? In fact, the damage will be so severe that you cannot take full responsibility; this is how severe the issue is. Even if you, yourself, did not live an evil life, if your philosophy was wrong, the negative influence it will have on people will be huge. This is highly risky work. That is why it is important to be mindful of the kind of thoughts you harbor, which is something we have been warning about many, many times.

Many of the angels who have fallen to hell were religious leaders when they were alive. Many religious leaders in Japan have fallen to hell as well. Even now, they are continuing to fall. All kinds of things can happen, such as their teachings may have been right but ended up being wrong along the way. Some went astray from their original mission or gave in to evil spirits somewhere in their lives. People sometimes lose against them. It is sad, but sometimes they lose in an all-out battle. Happy Science also has vulnerable times, such as when it is expanding or faced with financial difficulties. What will happen when we are attacked during those times? This is the crucial point. It would be best if we could come together as one and defend our group, but if not, it would be disastrous.

A few other religious groups recently lost their battles. Last summer, a religious leader of a group with two million members died and went straight to hell. In a case like that, nothing can be done. He cannot be saved. I cannot save him, either. I cannot save a person who had wrongly influenced the minds of over two million people. It is quite impossible. Unless the believers of the group return to the other world, complete their discipline and be reborn, nothing can be done. This is the outcome he will have to suffer.

As for Darwin, he was not a hypocritical man, but his philosophy contained bad seeds. The question is, what kinds of fruit did the seeds he planted bear in later years? It is sad but true that his philosophy has led to the movement of denying God. If the fruit was bad, then there must have been an issue with its seed or origin. He must take responsibility for this part. For him to be saved, a person who can refute his theories must appear. This is the only way he will be saved. If he has any virtue, I'm sure his soul friend would come down to demolish and eliminate his theory. Then, he may be saved. This is the tough situation he is in.

In this earthly world, people cannot tell the difference between what is good and what is bad just as the saying goes, "gems and stones in a hopeless jumble." Even to this day, university professors are teaching Marxian economics. What will happen to those whose lives were all about researching this philosophy? When they return to the other world, no one will be able to convince them that what they had been studying was all wrong. Even a monk will be unable to persuade them. They will have lived several decades believing in Marxism, so of course, they will not be able to let go of it. This is the sad truth. That is why choosing what to believe in puts a lot at stake in your life. If you choose to believe in the wrong philosophy, you will suffer the consequences, so you must be prepared.

Anyway, it is of no use to be talking about others, so please focus on yourself. You must start with yourself. Watch your own steps, not others—this is the deciding factor for most people, in other words, the ordinary people. You may point at famous philosophers and say, "That's how he ended up," but most people will not become famous and influential philosophers. So, please focus on your own thoughts and actions first.

CHAPTER THREE

Eternal Life and Life Training

1
The Meaning of Suffering

Q1

I would like to ask about the meaning of suffering in this world. Some spiritual beings say, "If you are suffering, it means you have a hellish mindset. Therefore, suffering is something that no one should experience to begin with." However, great artists and historical figures from the past became who they were after overcoming setbacks and suffering. So, I feel that immersing oneself in suffering and sadness also plays a crucial role in helping the soul grow and increase its caliber. I would be grateful if you could tell us how we should view suffering. Should we reject suffering and ignore it completely or is that a wrong approach to move forward?

The Fifth Lecture of 1989, "New Developments in Success Theory"
Held on July 16, 1989 at Hotel Nagoya Castle in Aichi, Japan

Two ways of dealing with suffering

OK, I understand. When considering this, we must not forget that each person is guided and taught in the way that is most suitable for them. There are 3,200 people here at my lecture today, so if I were to guide every person in the way that is most suitable to them, the number of different teachings would be immeasurable. So, it is important to consider which aspect of the Truth you will emphasize.

There are two ways to deal with suffering as you have mentioned in your question, and both of them are in line with the Truth. They do not contradict the Truth. Suffering is a real phenomenon. It exists. And when it comes, most people think, "Things are not going the way I want. It pains my soul." I, too, go through days like this, of course.

However, the outcome for each person depends on how they deal with their challenges. If people learn from their challenges and level up as human beings, it means that they gained nourishment for the soul from their painful experiences. Their soul will start shining. This is an approach that I currently teach, which I call Invincible Thinking. I believe this is a relatively natural approach to take when facing challenges in this third dimensional world.

Another way to approach suffering is to think, "There is essentially no suffering, no evil, and nothing to worry about. Thinking that these things exist is hellish thinking and no one should think this way. We must believe in the monism of light, the monism of joy." This approach can be a great form of love if you see it in a different light. How so? The role of suffering, of course, is to teach people or nourish their souls in the way that I just mentioned, but the majority of people tend to get too caught up in it. Worries can help people develop themselves, but as they delve into them, they tend to suffer even more and become consumed by them. When this happens, what these people need are the following words of encouragement: "Essentially, there is no suffering. Suffering is not actually real. You are an existence of light. You originally came from a world of light. Humans, in reality, shine like a diamond." When a person hears these words, they can quickly detach themselves from their unnecessary self-blaming thoughts. This is similar to how people attain enlightenment in Zen meditation. It is a mentality that helps people come back from the abyss of suffering. It is indeed true.

People who are strong enough to confront these negative thoughts and detach themselves from them, in other words, those who believe in the Power of Self, are fine as they are. But you need to take a different approach with people who are drowning in their suffering. It is better to offer these people gentle and simple teachings that will remove their suffering. Some people truly feel their worries dissolve when they are told, "Do not be attached to your suffering. It does not exist in reality. There is only joy. The true nature of humans is Light." So, we cannot ignore the effectiveness of this approach. We cannot completely abandon it.

Some of you in the audience here today are very distinguished souls, perhaps bodhisattvas. But even beings like bodhisattvas experienced much suffering in the past. They tend to focus too much on their suffering, which is a habit they developed over their reincarnations. That is why they have complicated thought processes and agonize over their worries. This can of course lead to spiritual growth. However, let me just tell you this. When you are too caught up in your own problems, you forget to pay attention to other people. You will not be able to give love to others, help them when they are in need, or prevent them from getting into trouble. So, you should spend less time thinking about yourself and, instead, focus your energy on shedding light on other people. This is a very rational teaching.

To conclude, I think that both of these ways of approaching suffering are in line with the Truth. It is just a matter of how each person interprets their suffering.

Relative dualism: why God allows suffering to exist

As for my views on suffering, I look at it from the viewpoint of relative dualism. I wrote about this in the book, *The Laws of Eternity* (New York: IRH Press, 2024). In the book, I said, "Spirits in the realms close to the third dimensional world experience suffering and sadness, but they are only allowed to exist as ingredients to improve their souls as children of God and shine the divine light that they originally have. Suffering should be used for this purpose."

The higher up you go in the dimensions, meaning the higher up you go in the world of light, the less suffering and sadness you will feel. But suffering and sadness will not completely disappear as long as your soul retains a human character. As long as you are a human, you will naturally shed tears. In the same way, emotions such as joy and sadness will remain with you for as long as you are a human soul with a human character. Because of this, we can say that sadness and suffering will never end. It will always be there while you are expressing yourself as a soul with a human character.

If you prefer to view this world as a place filled with happiness and joy, then you can pursue the idea that only light exists. I will not deny it. That is one of the paths you can take, so go ahead. That is my answer.

From the third dimensional perspective, suffering indeed exists. But whether you view sadness and suffering as lessons

The Laws of Eternity (New York: IRH Press, 2024)

to learn from, or turn a blind eye to them and look toward a bright future, is simply a difference in approach. Both approaches are expedient. It is just a matter of which one is easier for you to understand, nothing more. In fact, those who preach positive thinking are aware of the dark side of suffering, but they know that if they focus too much on it, their believers will end up becoming preoccupied with it.

A good example of this is whether you educate people by praising or scolding them. Both approaches are in line with the Truth. If people only receive praise, they will become too easy on themselves. They will end up becoming spoiled, so it is not good to be overly lenient. On the other hand, if people are scolded constantly, they will become negative and passive. So, both praising and scolding are needed for people to grow in a balanced way.

Likewise, there are two aspects to the Laws and the teachings as well. Sometimes, people need to be taught lessons so they realize what is evil and wrong. At other times, they need to be taught what is truly wonderful. Both aspects balance out the teachings. This is what I think.

But on an individual level, those with a brighter view of life, who focus more on the positives, are happier. So, I recommend that everyone take on a positive view of life.

2
The Meaning of Death

Q2

My friend who I used to study the Truth with passed away three days ago. She had a lung infection a few months ago, and when the doctors checked the dark spot in her lungs, it turned out to be malignant. After the surgery was scheduled, she prayed for 10 days, and because she had such strong faith in your teachings, the dark spot disappeared. She was then discharged.

Before she went home, she even did missionary work by writing a letter and giving it to her doctor, along with one of your books. But two days later, she had an asthma attack and died from breathing difficulties.

I want to ask, why did heaven have to take her away just when she had become truly determined to do missionary work?

The First Lecture of 1990, "Faith and Love"
Held on March 11, 1990 at Makuhari Messe, Chiba, Japan

Each person has their own destiny

A person's days in this world are pre-determined. To the people in the earthly world, death is a misfortune, but to the spirits in the other world, it is a new birth. The death of a person on earth is the birth of a new teammate in heaven. To the beings in heaven, seeing souls return after living out their lives and completing their mission in this world is like celebrating a birthday or an admission into school. They welcome the souls back by saying, "You're finally home!"

Each person has their own fate, so nobody has a right to make judgments about it. Some people die early while others live longer, but that is up to their destiny. Just because you have a pure heart does not mean you will live for hundreds of years. Nor do people with an impure heart necessarily die early. Each person has a rough schedule outlined for their life training on earth. Most of it is planned out. Of course, there are times when your destiny or plan is rewritten. But I believe that your friend has an important mission that awaits her—a mission that outweighs your wish for her destiny to change. She has work to do in heaven.

In my case, for example, because I am now living in this world, I cannot manage the work I'm in charge of in the Real World, which is creating problems. This is the reality. There is work in the Real World that cannot be done while I am living in this world. With this in mind, we can understand the thoughts of the spirits in heaven. On the one hand, they are cheering on people's spiritual training in this world, but on the other hand, they want them to come back as soon as possible. In fact, spirits in heaven say to me, "We need you to come back to heaven soon. We're having trouble getting the work done." So, each person's lifespan is determined by these two factors.

As for your friend, she lived courageously and you saw her live that way. This memory of her will live on eternally in your heart, so you should take on her spirit and work hard doing missionary activities while you live in this world. At the same time, you can pray for your friend so that she will be successful in carrying out her real mission in heaven. People who lived righteously will undoubtedly be in charge of a far more important mission when they return to the other world, so this is something to congratulate her on. I am certain that her death was a calling from heaven to carry out her mission there.

3

How to Effectively Study and Practice the Truth in the Time You Have Remaining

Q3

Earlier, in your lecture, you mentioned that humans have eternal life, which I, too, believe.

Considering how much time I have left until I reach 80 years old, one way for me to live from now on is to spend the first 10 years building a foundation by learning the Truth and the remaining 10 years spreading the Truth to other people. The only issue is that, because I only started studying the Truth recently, I feel that the most I can do in this life of 70 or 80 years is to study the Truth.

So my plan for this lifetime is to study the Truth, and I will make the wisdom I gain blossom in my next life. Could you please tell me your thoughts on a long-term life plan that includes the next life and the life after that?

The Fifth Public Lecture of 1989, "New Developments in Success Theory"
Held on July 16, 1989 at Hotel Nagoya Castle in Aichi, Japan

The importance of accomplishing what you can in this life

I might be wrong, but do you mean that you have more or less given up on your current life? I have only just started publishing books, so if people are already giving up on studying them, I will lose my motivation and energy to publish more. From around this spring, I have been rapidly receiving thoughts of people thinking, "I can't keep up with the reading," and I have struggled to write books since then. So, I hope people will be more eager to read. I want people to say, "I want to study the Truth more." This will give me more energy to write.

After hearing what you just said, I will be publishing one less book [*laughs*]. I'm just kidding. In any case, it is too early for you to give up. Humans are capable of improving their ability as much as they want. So, what you need to do is to work on improving your ability. You still have a few more decades of life to live. I would understand if you only have a few days left to live, but you still have a long way to go, so please do not give up. Be more hungry for the Truth. I even want you to say, "Is that all you've got? Is that all the Laws you can preach? Teach us more."

I understand that it is impossible for you to tell people about all of the teachings. So, focus on the topic that you are good at or confident in and share that with other people. As for the other topics, you do not have to go into too much depth when you are studying them. There is a limit to how much you can absorb, which is an undeniable fact. So, try to study the various teachings, but you do not have to go too deep into all of them. For the topics you are good at, delve into them and practice them. Please do this. I'm sure you can do it. You definitely can. It is possible. We are also planning to follow up on people who are struggling to learn the Truth by providing them with different study methods. I will teach you many efficient ways to study and practice the teachings, so please leave it up to me.

In any case, please remember that you will only accomplish as much as the effort you put in, so give it your all in this life. It is too early for you to be thinking about your next life or the life after that. You can think about that after you return to the Real World. Please give it your best in this lifetime.

Further, the more eager you are to seek the Truth, the higher your chances of being born in an age when the Truth is taught. The stronger your enthusiasm in this lifetime, the more likely you will be born into such an age in your next life. People who think, "I'll just make an effort in my next life" will often repeat the same mistake they made in this life in their next life. So, please do everything you can. You can definitely do that.

4
The Problem with Thinking That "A Cause Is Immediately Followed by a Result"

Q4

Are the law of cause and effect (*inga* 因果) and karma (*in'nen* 因縁) the same thing?

Special Public Seminar, "Heaven and Hell"
Held on April 26, 1992 at Sendai Sunplaza in Miyagi, Japan

Inga refers to "cause and effect" whereas *in'nen* refers to "cause and condition"

In a broad sense, the law of cause and effect (*inga* 因果) and karma (*in'nen* 因縁) both have the same meaning. There isn't much difference. In our teachings, we often use the words "cause and effect," "karma" and "causality (*engi* 縁起)." *Engi* is an abbreviation for *in'nen shoki*(因縁生起). In any case, you can consider them all the same in a broad sense.

The Japanese kanji character for karma is *in'nen* (因縁), which is made up of *in* (因) meaning cause, and *en* (縁) meaning condition. On the other hand, kanji for cause and effect is *inga* (因果), which is made up of *in* (因) meaning cause, and *ka* or *ga* (果) meaning effect. If we look closely at the words, *in'nen* just focuses on the cause and the condition required for the cause to bring about the effect. So the effect is not included in the word, *in'nen*. On the other hand, *inga* means the cause and the effect. So, there is a slight difference between the two words, which is whether the process between cause and effect is included or not.

To explain in terms of how a plant grows, *in* is the seed and *en* is the process of adding water, nutrients, and light to the seed. Then, as a result, a flower will bloom. So, *in'nen* focuses on the seed and the condition; it says, "There is a seed, and when this seed is given nutrients, water, and light, a flower blooms." On the other hand, *inga* says, "A seed will eventually grow into a flower." This is the difference. But essentially, the cause (*in*), the condition (*en*), and the result (*ga*) are all connected in the same flow of events. The difference between *inga* and *in'nen* is simply which two of the three elements are being focused on.

To achieve a result, you must not ignore the effort

However, you must be careful with the word *inga* or cause and effect. You must not take it simply and just think that a cause will immediately lead to a result. This kind of thinking creates problems. Religious organizations that emphasize positive thinking too much often use this type of thinking. A certain religious group in Japan teaches that a cause will instantly produce results. But this is the same as saying that you can become a tathagata with a single leap. It is extreme to think, "A cause will instantly produce results. As long as you sow a seed, a flower will undoubtedly bloom."

It is easy to say that people can become a tathagata by thinking like a tathagata, and indeed, having the mind of a tathagata is what makes you one. Buddhism often teaches that people can become a tathagata, in other words, buddha, because we all have the nature of a tathagata within. It sounds easy when we talk about it in terms of cause and effect, but in reality, it is not that simple. In between cause and effect comes the condition, and this corresponds to effort. When effort, or spiritual discipline, is added to the cause, it produces a result in the form of enlightenment. Any form of Buddhism that ignores this process of effort is not true Buddhism. I am very concerned that many of the Buddhist sects around the world don't teach this aspect of effort. They must not omit effort.

Some sects of Mahayana Buddhism implicitly teach people that a cause will instantly bring about an effect. This idea can be a seed of enlightenment and bear fruit for some people, but for most, it is not very helpful. For example, there is a teaching that says, "By chanting 'Amitabha Buddha,' you will be reborn in paradise"; this jumps straight from the cause to the result. It downplays the process. This is more or less the same as saying, "As long as you head west, you will reach Tokyo." While this may be true, it is not so easy to get there with just this instruction. All it says is to head west to get to Tokyo, but it is not that simple because you actually need to take detailed, specific paths to get there.

The teaching of spiritual discipline is meaningless if you don't consider the process. Those that focus on Self-power tend to put more weight on the process while those that focus more on Other-power tend to ignore it. In one of the Buddhist Schools called the Consciousness-Only School, there is a doctrine of permeation (*kunjyu*). It means "learning that you gain over time will permeate your soul," which is like what happens when food is smoked and comes with deep flavor, or when you light incense and its scent permeates the room. Similarly, when you keep making efforts, the lessons you gain from experience will permeate your soul. This is the doctrine of permeation, which explains why the condition is necessary. Another word for *kunjyu* is *jikke*, which means something similar and also focuses on the condition. *Jikke* means the permeation of experience.

Just because there is a cause does not mean results will appear instantly. In between the two are processes such as *kunjyu* and *jikke*, which mean getting used to your training and letting your experience permeate through to your soul. Only after that will the results appear. This process of permeation means studying, putting in effort, and gaining experience in this world. It is important that you have this way of thinking.

Your question was on cause and effect and cause and karma, so I hope you got a better idea of those two concepts by listening to my explanation. They both mean the same thing, but the important part is the condition that joins the cause and effect. Without it, Buddhism would not be Buddhism in the truest sense. Please understand this point well. I will talk about this topic in more depth. I hope you all study hard together.

5
How to Convey the Truth to Atheists

Q5

While some people think that God or Buddha and the other world may exist, others do not believe in God or Buddha in the slightest. How can I give love and convey the Truth to those people by practicing the ultimate form of self-realization?

The Fourth Public Lecture of 1989, "The Ultimate Self-Realization"
Held on July 8, 1989 at Sonic City in Saitama, Japan

Be understanding toward people who have yet to awaken to the Truth

Your question has to do with the true meaning of "love that gives." People view others relative to themselves; they view them through their own mirror. If the image of a person reflected in your mirror is crooked, you will want to correct it. But before you do, you need to consider whether your mirror is truly polished and not dented or crooked.

For example, if I were to look into a convex mirror on a pillar, I would look quite different. I might have distorted ears or a vertically long face. In a concave mirror, my reflection will also be warped but perhaps in a different way. As you can see from this example, the reflected image of a person varies depending on the type of mirror used. So, although you see many kinds of people and think that some are atheists who don't believe in God, you must first be aware that the image of the person you are seeing is not their entire being. Likewise, the image of you that the other person sees will not be complete, either. It will likely be distorted. You must first acknowledge this point before conveying the Truth. Please know this. Once you do, you will become more understanding toward others. To be understanding is to be forgiving toward people who have yet to awaken to the Truth. Forgiveness is another form of love and is synonymous with being understanding.

Since you are not a "perfect mirror," others may appear crooked to you. Perhaps, it is you who do not see their wonderful aspects. You may look at some people and one-sidedly judge them to be living against God's Will, but their lifestyle could actually be consistent with it. Even among people who do not believe in God, many may be living in the way that God wishes them to. Some of them are actually doing better than you in certain aspects. So first, please be aware of this fact. Being understanding toward others is the first prerequisite.

Consider whether it is the right time for the other person

The second point I want to mention is that there is a right time for each person to encounter the Truth. Also, there is a different level of intensity to how much each person is seeking the Truth. These are facts.

Take a meal, for example. A meal will not taste good if it is not served at the right time. Your lunch will not taste good if you have had a late breakfast. Likewise, people have the right time to encounter the Truth. No matter how many times you may try to convey the Truth to someone, if the time is not right for them, you will only leave them with a faint impression. On the contrary, even if you are not passionately conveying the Truth, if the time is right for someone, it will deeply seep into their mind.

So, the first prerequisite is to be understanding and the second prerequisite is to consider whether it is the right time for the other person, not when it is right for you. "When would be the right time for them? Is it now? Will it come in a year?" In this way, I would like you to wait for the appropriate time. Sometimes, it may seem as though the right time for the person will never come during your lifetime. That is beyond your control. In that case, please pray for their happiness in your mind. They have a guardian spirit, so pray to their guardian spirit in your mind in the following way: "Please be sure to give them a chance to awaken to the Truth." You do not have to let the other person know that you have done this.

Some people will reject you when you try to teach them about God. This means that it is not the right time for them yet. Moreover, you may not be given the chance to be around that person when the right time comes for them. In that case, although you may be rejected, do not let it scar you. Instead, pray to the person's guardian spirit by thinking, "Please make sure this person learns the Truth appropriately when the time comes." This will be enough.

Be mindful of how strongly the person is in need of the Truth

The third point is to be mindful of how strongly the person is in need of the Truth. When someone is seeking the Truth as strongly as you (the questioner) are, you must teach them accordingly. But for people who are not seeking as strongly, you must simplify the Truth in accordance with what they need.

Some people do not believe in God or Buddha but understand love. If not love, they may understand kindness or friendliness. Perhaps they will understand love if you tell them it means to put yourself in someone else's shoes. They will not be able to argue with you about that. If you tell them, "You should practice 'love that gives,'" they may say, "I don't believe in that," but they may understand if you tell them, "It is important for you to put yourself in other people's shoes." As you can see, there are many different ways you can tell people the Truth.

It is very important to be able to break down difficult ideas and explain them simply. This is very much related to the level of your enlightenment. The more enlightened you become, the more you can explain high-level teachings in simple words. It is easy to explain high-level teachings using difficult words to people with high-level souls. But what matters more is how simply you can explain the Truth. You can do this to match the level of a person's soul. If you are talking about "love that gives," you could explain it as being friendly or kind to others. You could say that it means to put yourself in other people's shoes. You could even say that it means not to flaunt how kind you have been to others. In this way, there are various ways to explain the Truth.

What is important is to take on the Truth, make it your own philosophy, and share it with others at the appropriate time. You do not have to say that it is my philosophy or my teaching. Please tell people the Truth as your own thinking. Share the Truth in a way that is comfortable for you and that fits the other person. That is more than enough. If they can understand even a fraction of what you say, that is enough. Just be mindful of the three points I mentioned.

6
Life Training for Bodhisattvas-to-be

Q6

In one of your early lectures, you said that you would nurture 1,000 arhats (Refer to "The Principle of Happiness" compiled as Chapter One in *The Ten Principles from El Cantare Volume 1* [New York: IRH Press, 2021]). You have also taught us that there are steps to becoming an arhat, which is to first become a hearer and then a solitary realizer. What is the difference between the state of mind of a solitary realizer and an arhat?

Also, is it possible for someone who is training to become an arhat to practice acts of a bodhisattva? Please teach us about the relationship between the practice of a bodhisattva and the discipline to become an arhat.

The Second Special Lecture of 1990, "The Spirit of Missionary Work"
Held on September 2, 1990 at Kitakyushu City Gymnasium in Fukuoka, Japan

The difference between a hearer, a solitary realizer, and an arhat

OK, I understand.

Hearer and solitary realizer are old Buddhist terms, so they may not sound familiar to people today. Let me explain them more simply in modern language. A hearer, or *shomon* (声聞) in Japanese kanji characters, is written as "listening (聞) to the voice (声)," so a hearer refers to someone like you (the questioner) who is here today. It refers to someone with the attitude needed to come and listen to the teachings of the Truth. More than 7,000 people from Kyushu and other parts of Japan are attending this event today. Having a desire to listen to the Truth, in itself, is certainly not ordinary but a rare and remarkable wish to have. Having this mindset alone shows that you are all one step ahead of other people. This is the state of a hearer. People who enjoy listening to a lecture on the Truth, either in person or on a cassette tape [or CD or DVD], have reached this state.

In contrast, those who have reached the level of a solitary realizer are aware of their mission. At the level of a hearer, you are happy with just hearing the Truth; your mind and soul are in a state of joy. However, when you reach the state of a solitary realizer, you begin to think about your mission and the purpose of your soul in this lifetime. You will find that just listening to the Truth does not satisfy you; you will want to find out about your soul's mission and develop yourself through spiritual discipline or other means. When you awaken to this sense of mission, you will transition from a hearer to a solitary realizer. A solitary realizer, or *engaku* (縁覚) in kanji, is written as "awakening (覚) to fate (縁)." Fate refers to your destiny of meeting Buddha's Truth or meeting God. When you awaken to it, you will become a solitary realizer.

The level above a solitary realizer is called an arhat. Arhats are those who have entered the path of spiritual discipline; usually, they are already on the path. They are studying the Truth and are making efforts in pursuit of enlightenment. To become an arhat, you must have an aspiration for enlightenment. Those with this aspiration have a strong yearning to attain enlightenment and are making diligent efforts toward it. So, an arhat has a very clear goal. A solitary realizer, on the other hand, has yet to reach that level. An arhat can clearly see the direction in which they should head to attain enlightenment.

There are two levels to an arhat: arhat-in-training (阿羅漢向 *arakan-ko*) and arhat-attained (阿羅漢果 *arakan-ka*). Arhat-in-training is the state in which you are still on your way to becoming an arhat. Arhat-attained is the state in which you have reached the arhat state and can maintain the mind of an arhat. Most people who study the Truth and attend various Happy Science events will more or less reach the state of arhat-in-training. For instance, if you become a regular member of Happy Science (now called a devotee member), read 10 books of Truth, and attend seminars and study sessions, you will most likely reach the state of arhat-in-training in a short time. This is possible as long as you are not burdened by any major problems and have completed some level of self-reflection. After you have done this for two to three years, you can reach the arhat-attained state, where your mind rarely wavers.

During those two to three years, you will experience many things. You may have been doing fine on your own until, one day, your friend gets into trouble or starts attacking you. From there, all kinds of problems may occur. Things like this can happen in two to three years and can cause your mind to waver. They may cause you to drop out even after reaching the state of arhat. So, to enter the state of arhat-attained, you must be able to persevere through various hardships without dropping out so easily.

How to become a true bodhisattva

To take a step further and go beyond the state of arhat-attained, you need to reach the indomitable state. An arhat is still at the level of being satisfied with just pursuing individual enlightenment. But when an arhat reaches the next stage, the indomitable state, their spiritual level rises and they awaken to a greater mission rather than merely focusing on their personal growth. They will focus more on this greater mission than on their personal mission. They will begin to have thoughts such as, "What does the current age call for? What is God calling for? What are people seeking now? What is needed now?" They will awaken to God's ideal. When they realize that the great mission and the spiritual discipline they have been undergoing are connected, they become determined. They come to think, "I shouldn't be bogged down by small, personal matters. Now is not the time. I must work harder." When they reach this state, nothing that others say, be it their family or friends, will make them waver. They will be able to repel them all. Why? It is because they have found out what their true mission is, what the world needs, and what God expects of them. It is because they have become aware of these things and embodied the great mission. They firmly believe that what they are doing is truly valuable. Because they have this unshakable belief, they become indomitable.

When you reach this indomitable state, it means you are at the entrance of becoming a bodhisattva. It is the first step of becoming a bodhisattva. So the difference between an arhat and a bodhisattva is whether a person has indomitable resolve. In other words, the question is whether you have awakened to a greater, public mission and fully made it your own. If your answer is yes, you have entered the state of bodhisattva.

To become a true bodhisattva, a person must become indomitable and courageously go forth and put their mission into practice. Through practice, they train themselves and develop their capacity to love and save more and more people. Only when they are able to do this—actually, when they are able to *continue* doing this—do they become a true bodhisattva. If you can feel that what you are doing is your calling, you will definitely be able to live out your earthly life as a bodhisattva and return to the world of bodhisattvas in the other world.

When bodhisattvas do missionary work, they love and save many people without seeking fame or any gain for themselves. They enjoy loving people, and seeing others become happy gives them joy. They believe that they were born to do this work. They naturally do missionary work as their calling, as their original mission, without straining themselves and being egoistic. Sharing the Truth they learned with others is only natural to them. They will naturally reach out their hand to those who are lost. They do it not because they are forced to or because someone told them that it is the right thing to do. They do it because they want to and because it comes naturally to them. Those who can maintain this state of mind for a very long time will become bodhisattvas.

This does not mean that an arhat cannot practice the acts of a bodhisattva. As a matter of course, while you are polishing your mind to become a bodhisattva, you will be given a training period, which is something everyone will go through. So, an arhat is someone who is not yet a bodhisattva but is in the training stage to become one. But if they keep clouding their minds while doing missionary work, they will regress from an arhat. As they do missionary work, various difficulties will arise. However, if they handle the difficulties well and overcome them, a new path will open. When an arhat gains enough abilities from difficult experiences, he or she will become a bodhisattva. The biggest difference between an arhat and a bodhisattva is that an arhat is still focused on personal development whereas a bodhisattva has completed this stage and is more focused on saving others.

This was a very general explanation, but I hope you understood me.

7

How to Attain the State of Absolute Love

Q7

You have taught us that having a selfless mind is a prerequisite to doing missionary work. But whenever I do missionary work or give love to others, I often end up thinking about myself and cannot seem to get away from the idea of relative love.

In *Spiritual Messages from Jesus Christ* (available only in Japanese), it says, "Love does not exist within what is relative; it exists within what is absolute." What is the difference between relative love and absolute love? Also, can you teach us how exactly we should practice and develop absolute love?

Special Seminar in Hokuriku, "A Lecture on *What Is Infinite Love?*"
Held on October 11, 1992 at Shinminato City Chuo Bunka Kaikan
in Toyama, Japan

Consider yourself a part of God's Work

Let me first explain the words "relative" and "absolute." In relative love, there is a clear distinction between the self and others. Those who practice relative love take credit for doing something for another person, thinking that it is thanks to them that the person is better and happy. So within them, there is a very clear distinction between self and others. In other words, they still think, "It is thanks to me..." Those who have this strong sense of self and others tend to think, "He seems happy so it means I did a good job." This is the meaning of relative love.

On the other hand, the self disappears in absolute love. As it has been said from long ago, when you see yourself as the hands and feet of God, when you feel that God is doing missionary work through you, or when you feel that your work is just a part of God's Work, you are practicing something absolute. So, you will not take credit for what you do and you will not think, "It is thanks to me that he got better."

Let's say that you convey the Truth to someone and their situation gets better. It could be that their family situation improves, they develop a better relationship within their family, they establish a happy marriage, or they succeed in their work. Various things may happen, and as a result, they may thank you for it. I wouldn't say it is completely wrong to be joyful and think, "I'm so glad that it went well." That is fine. But in such moments, if you can say without hesitation, "No, it wasn't me. It wasn't my doing. I didn't guide you. It was the work of God or the power of God," then you are practicing absolute love. This is the ideal.

It is very hard not to take credit for your achievements in missionary work when you are giving your all. You feel proud of yourself and want to boast about your success to others. When you are thanked by people, you may start feeling that you want to be appreciated even more. But instead of feeling that way, try to think, "This is not my doing. God is allowing me to do it." This is an important point. As long as you stay humble, you will be able to do even greater work. But if you take the credit for yourself, the opposite will happen.

Unfortunately, we feel unaccomplished and unsatisfied unless we receive rewards for our work. That is human nature. So, it is OK to feel some degree of accomplishment. But as a religious spirit gradually sinks deep into your body and takes root in your soul, you will come to think, "God is working through me." If you can say, "It is God's work, not mine" to the person you are conveying the Truth to, they will make further progress. Please tell them, "I am not the one that helped you. It was God's doing. Because I have a spiritual connection with you, God used me to help you awaken to your mission, whatever it may be. So, instead of thanking me, thank God and return the favor to God. You can do that by giving love to others as I have done to you. This is what it means to give back to God." It is very important to have this kind of mentality.

8

The Mindset to Have in an Age of Crisis

Q8

Some of the spiritual message books from Happy Science clearly state that an age of crisis will come. I would appreciate it if you could teach us the mindset that people joining Happy Science should have and give us a specific guide for action in the coming age of crisis.

The Third Lecture of 1989, "The Secret of the Multidimensional Universe"
Held on May 28, 1989 at Kobe Port Island Hall in Hyogo, Japan

Always stick to Invincible Thinking

I know that both Happy Science members and non-members are in the audience today, but this answer will be strictly for our members. What I want to say to them is, "Do not be attached to your physical life." What I mean is that we are not carrying out our activities to survive the age of crisis. Please listen carefully. Being a Happy Science member, you may receive information promptly, such as which particular region will be likely to sink, and therefore be able to escape before everyone else and survive. But that should not be the reason you became a member. Even if this venue were to sink, it is our mission to do everything we can until the very end. Natural disasters are indeed expected to happen, but that should not hold us back. They are expected to happen in other countries, too, but that should not stop us. Rather, it is all the more urgent for us to go to places where disasters are likely to happen.

After all, our life on earth is limited. It is finite. So for me, it makes little difference whether I leave this world earlier or later. Whether I die earlier or later is not my concern. Rather, what is important for each person is how many lessons a person gains in this lifetime and how much work they do before they die.

So, no matter what kind of crisis befalls us, we do not need to panic. I am sure there are non-members here, too, but let me tell you this: Times of great confusion and times of countless natural disasters are also great opportunities for us to spread the Truth. Natural disasters are expected to occur in many foreign countries and they are precisely where I want to build our branches, send our lecturers, and carry out missionary work. If those places sink, you will just have to swim your way back home, that's all. I want our members to have this kind of mentality. You are studying the eternal Truth, so please do not lose your composure over a mere earthquake, lightning, a fire, or "your old man." Your life will not end. Rather, I hope you will think of such a time as an opportunity to make full use of your abilities and be determined to fulfill your mission.

Let me repeat myself. Please do not be attached to your physical life. That is all I have to say. Please do not lose your composure. People who understand the Truth must remain calm in times of crisis. Awakened people must stand firm in times when everyone else is panicking. We need calm people.

No matter what the situation is, Happy Science will always stick to Invincible Thinking. We must always draw the best possible results from tough situations without being swayed by them. This is how we, Happy Science, think and act.

CHAPTER FOUR

The Reality of the Great Universe and Time from the Perspective of God

1

The Transformation of Planets into Black Holes as Seen by God

Q1

In the past, you have taught us that a planet has a lifespan of about 15 billion years and that it will eventually turn into a black hole and die. However, based on modern scientific theory, I know that a planet needs to be at least twice the size of the Sun for it to become a black hole. Could you please explain the process or system of how a planet turns into a black hole?

The Third Lecture of 1989, "Secrets of the Multidimensional Universe"
Held on May 28, 1989 at Kobe Port Island Hall in Hyogo, Japan

Considering a planet as a single life form

A planet does not necessarily have to be twice the size of the Sun for it to become a black hole. Earth has the potential to turn into a black hole, too. Although it has a diameter of about 1/109 of the Sun, if Earth were to be compressed to half the size of my thumb, it would turn into a black hole. You will find this to be true if you do the calculations based on physics. When you compress the volume of something with a mass as big as a planet down to such a small size, it becomes a black hole. This is because the planet's gravitational pull becomes stronger than its outward pressure and begins to warp time and space around it. The compressed planet then begins to absorb light and other things. So, a planet does not have to be so big for it to become a black hole.

There are a few ways to explain the phenomenon of a planet becoming a black hole. One is that it is the end of a planet's life. When you consider a planet as a single life form, you can say that it becomes a black hole at the end of its life. In the case of humans, we repeatedly go through reincarnation by dwelling in a physical body, but only consciousnesses up to the ninth dimension do so. In the case of tenth dimensional consciousnesses, also known as planetary consciousnesses, they undergo soul training by dwelling in planetary bodies.

As for planet Earth, an enormous consciousness called the Earth Consciousness dwells in it. The round ball we call Earth is not a lump of dirt but a body, and within it dwells a planetary consciousness called the Earth Consciousness. However, if a planetary consciousness, in this case the Earth Consciousness, were to remain as it is forever, it would eventually stop evolving. That is why Earth must die at some point. In this way, planets also go through a cycle of reincarnation. Their cycle is much, much longer compared to that of human beings; it takes 10 or 20 billion years per cycle. Nonetheless, a planet certainly goes through birth and death.

A planet can die in one of a few ways, which are very similar to the way human beings die. For instance, someone may die when they get into an accident. For a planet, this corresponds to a planetary collision. This is how some planets disappear. Another way someone could die is from an illness. The closest thing to that for a planet is a black hole where the planet itself grows weak. Just as a person loses weight and grows weak when they develop cancer, a planet shrinks when it weakens. We would not be able to witness this within our lifetime because a planet shrinks over a very long period of time, but it "loses weight" like a cancer patient does. And when the planet's time of death is determined, it usually turns into a black hole. From the perspective of an onlooker, it is a very interesting spectacle. It is like watching a pickled plum shrivel up as it dries. A planet shrinks in a similar fashion over millions and billions of years. This is how a planet turns into a black hole. We can presume that there are entities in charge of the birth and death of planets. There must be beings who are making planets reincarnate.

So, it is wrong to say that a planet must be twice the size of our Sun for it to turn into a black hole. However, in the case of a small planet, it is probably more likely to disappear as a result of a collision.

2

The Effect That Other Planets Have on Earth

Q2

Please teach us how the planets in the Solar System were created and the spiritual and physical effect they have on planet Earth and humanity.

The Ninth Lecture of 1990, "The Enlightenment on the Great Universe"
Held on August 26, 1990 at Makuhari Messe in Chiba, Japan

A planet is born in one of three ways

Broadly speaking, a planet is born in one of three ways. The first is when it shoots out explosively or pops out from a ball of light or heat like the Sun in our Solar System. This is what happened with Earth and Mercury.

Another is the way Venus was born. When Mercury shot out from the Sun about seven billion years ago, many small asteroids popped out at the same time. There were other objects flying through space, too. These small asteroids and other astronomical objects then came together and formed Venus. When you witness this process from a spiritual perspective, you will see that there is a core and that various things gather around the core under a single purpose. In the third dimensional sense, this may seem as though gravity is at work.

The last way in which a planet can be born is when gases and dust come together and form a ball of mass. Once this ball of mass grows to a certain size, it begins to take on a purpose and develops a gravitational pull. All kinds of things are attracted into its gravitational field and, when they crash into each other, massive amounts of energy are released, which leads to the formation of new matter. So, as the ball further increases in size, it takes on a will and works to achieve a certain purpose. Now that it has will, it eventually develops into a planet.

On another note, although planets look spherical to us, in reality, some are not. For example, Phobos, a natural satellite of Mars, is full of bumps and dips. There are many other celestial objects like this in outer space. In fact, Phobos is an asteroid caught in the gravitational pull of Mars. It was not there originally but as it flew through space, it was captured in Mars' gravitational field. That is how it came to orbit Mars.

So, as I have explained, a planet can form in one of several ways. In the case of our Solar System, a planet can be formed as a result of combining small debris that scatter when another planet shoots out of the Sun and rock-type objects that fly through space.

The lessons learned from soul training on other planets affect the evolution of Earth

Now, let me explain from another viewpoint, that is, from the perspective of spiritual influence. As I wrote in *The Laws of the Sun*, Earth is not the only planet on which human-like beings have lived. As an experiment, human-like beings have lived on other planets as well, which is something I haven't explained in detail yet.

Take Venus, for example. It currently has an atmospheric pressure of about 90 atm and its surface temperature is about 400 degrees Celsius. Venus is also reported to have very little water. But until about one billion years ago, it had been a planet of lush vegetation with rivers flowing through it. Venus was therefore a planet with plentiful water, but as it continued to be exposed to radiation from the Sun, gases like carbon dioxide and water vapor were produced. As they pooled in the atmosphere, it led to a greenhouse effect,

The Laws of the Sun
(New York: IRH Press, 2018)

which caused the surface temperature to rise. Eventually, there came a point at which living creatures could no longer survive. There was such a time on Venus about one billion years ago.

Prior to this, the environment of Venus was similar to that of modern-day Earth and many creatures had lived there. As it is written in *The Laws of the Sun*, human-like beings called Venusians had lived there as well as beings who came from other planets. Such a situation was not only the case for Venus but also for Mars. Humans may even live on Mars in the future as its environment is not too different from the environment on Earth. I think it is very likely that humans will live there in times to come.

As I have explained, from the perspective of spiritual influence, each planet has its own mission. Earth is not the only planet on which life forms can be nurtured. Each planet has its own purpose, and different times call for soul training on different planets. Although soul training may not be taking place on some planets at the moment, the fact that it did in the past is recorded in the "grand thought tape" of the entire Solar System which is similar to the thought tape that humans have. In other words, the planets in our Solar System have a common consciousness. It retains a record or a memory of the soul training that took place on those planets. This memory affects the evolution of Earth in some way.

As life flourishes on Earth, spiritual life forms that have lived on other planets become attracted to Earth. The souls of these life forms may then be modified to fit their new life on Earth. In this way, there is an extremely close connection between Earth and other planets. However, this all happens over a span of billions of years, so it is an idea that is hard for you to relate to as a human being living right now.

3

The Secret of Time Created by God

Q3

My question is about the nature of time. You have taught us that time was created by God, but did this start with the Big Bang? Or was time already flowing before then? Does time only flow linearly from the past to the future, or does it loop around? If that is the case, how should we understand the concept of eternity? Furthermore, is there a different kind of time flowing in the 13th dimensional universe, which is very different from where we are?

Lastly, you have also taught us that time flows differently in the third dimension than it does in the fourth dimension and beyond. Does this mean that absolute time is the same but the concept is different in each dimension? Or does it mean that absolute time, itself, is different? I would appreciate it if you could answer these questions.

Chubu Region Special Seminar, "The Peaceful Mind"
Held on November 25, 1989 at Ichinomiya Community Hall in Aichi, Japan

Time flows differently depending on your soul training environment

OK, here are my answers.

Time is not constant. It is not uniform. Time flows differently depending on where you are in the universe and the environment of your soul training.

In the past, I gave a lecture on the book, *Messages from the Sun* (a two-part series, no longer in print) in which I talked about time. I will explain it to you again, here. Imagine concentric circles, and in the center lies the Will of God. The inner circles are worlds where beings close to God live and the outer circles are worlds like Earth where humans live. Now, from the center, draw a straight line outward, like a hand on a clock, and imagine this hand turning. The distance that the hand moves at the center of the circle is very small, but the distance covered by the tip of the hand is much larger. This is the concept of time.

So, at the origin of time is a brief thought. The thought springs forth in a moment, but that moment turns into an extremely long period of time toward the tip of the hand, which could be hundreds of millions, billions, or an even greater number of years. This is the difference in the way time moves in each dimension. The further out you go on the hand, the longer the relative time.

Let me explain how I know this. Your question is a little difficult for the many beginner-level learners of the Truth here today, so allow me to choose my words carefully. In the Spirit World, thoughts are realized very quickly. I know this from experience. In the spiritual world, the time it takes for a thought to manifest is extremely short. However, in this earthly world, it takes an extremely long time because time moves very slowly.

Nonetheless, even under these circumstances, sometimes results are attained very quickly in this world. For example, when a group of people living with the same beliefs get together and make a strong wish, it is realized in a very short time. This happens because a space that is not of the third dimension is created within this third dimension. To give you an idea, strong wishes made by a group of people with faith or people who are studying self-realization tend to manifest very quickly. But usually, in this world, it takes more time for thoughts to manifest into something.

What I mentioned above is one way to explain how time flows much faster in worlds that are further away from this one.

The power that allows the universe to exist is embedded in time

There is another issue regarding your understanding of time. You probably cannot help but think of time as something that is measured with a clock which, based on what I just talked about, is a judgment that people toward the "outer edge of the hand" make. In contrast, however, from the eyes of beings at the "center of the hand" or the origin of the universe, essentially, time does not exist. The reason for this is that time is a mode to express space. If time did not exist, there would be no way to express space.

What do I mean by that? Let me give you an example. There is the Sun and various things are orbiting around it; among them are planets on which life forms are living. What allows these things to exist in space is time. However, the word *time* is a term used by humans. At the root of time is simply the will that allows the universe to exist. What is this will or power that allows the universe and everything in it to exist? In fact, it is the power of love. It is the power of love that deems all things good and allows them to exist. So perhaps we are replacing the word *love* with *time*.

Just think about what would happen if the universe was completely still. What would be there? If time stopped and everything was still, what would become of this world? All three-dimensional existences would be expressed as nothing more than images on a photograph. In other words, this world would become like a world within a photograph. In a world like that, everything would freeze in its current state. There would be no freedom. There would be no potential for growth. However, by introducing time, all things can move, which means they can undergo development. They are allowed freedom. That is when love comes into play.

So, although it is a little difficult to understand, you should recognize that time and love are synonymous. They are the same thing.

4

The Wonders of Time in the Other World

Q4

How does time work in this world and the other world? Is there such a thing as time in the other world?

I think that by understanding the relationship between time in this world and time in the other world, we can get a clearer idea of how reincarnation works, so I would be grateful if you could teach us about that.

The Fourth Special Seminar of 1993,
"Lecture on *The Challenge of Enlightenment Vol. 1*"
Held on November 3, 1993 at Hotel Okura in Tokyo, Japan

In the other world, time is not measurable with a clock

In this world, time refers to something measured with the hands of a clock, but as you may have noticed, it works differently in the other world. Once you return to the other world, you will find that time is not something that is measured with a clock. Time exists differently depending on each spirit's level of insight. So, even among spirits in the other world, some cannot see the future at all because it is beyond their level of insight.

In the other world, time exists differently depending on the place. In some places, the past, present, and future are all one, while in other places, time is flowing. There are also places where time has stopped in the past, as well as futuristic places. What's more, there are places where time is in sync with the earthly world. In this way, time has multiple aspects in the other world. Basically, in the other world, time and space unfold in accordance with the spirits' level of awareness.

Let me give you an example of what I mean. In this world, we have finite space, like this venue where 2,000 people have gathered. We also have objective time, so we can say things like, "The lecture is from one o'clock to such-and-such a time." However, this is not how time and space work in the other world; they are both experienced subjectively. This means the notion of time and space changes, and can also warp in different ways, depending on the level of awareness a spirit has. Spirits who have an extremely high level of spiritual awareness may be able to travel to future worlds as well as to past worlds.

However, spirits whose awareness is not up to that level cannot travel through time and will continue to experience time and space like they did when they were alive. For example, those who practiced agriculture in a particular era when they were alive will continue to do so in the other world. If they grew mandarin oranges in a particular era in this world, they will continue to do so in the other world, too. I am not saying this is wrong. It just means that some spirits in the fifth dimension are living in a world where time has stood still. So within the fifth dimension, some spirits are living within a time loop and do not know that time has passed on earth. They have no awareness about the harvest on earth and are only concerned about their own, saying things like "We have a good harvest again this year." On the other hand, some spirits have more awareness and are acting as leaders and advising on the harvest within their dimension, all while observing the harvest turnout in the earthly world.

So, everything depends on the individual spirit. The awareness of time and space all depends on a spirit's level of insight. That is how it is in the other world.

Only "the order of events" and "the chain of cause and effect" exist in the other world

Although I can only explain it very generally, the "time" that people in this world refer to does not exist in the other world. Only "the order of events" and "the chain of cause and effect" exist. What came before an event and what comes after it is clear, but time, as we measure it in this world, does not exist.

In simple words, something that happened 100 years ago can appear like it is happening in the present. Even events that will happen in the future may appear as though they will happen very soon. Spirits in the other world do not wear a watch, so they wouldn't understand what we mean when we ask about time. To give an example, if a spirit experienced a shocking event 1,000 years ago, it would feel like the event is ongoing or happened just yesterday. But if it was an event that had little impact on the spirit, it would feel like it happened in the distant past. Time is quite subjective in this way in the other world. That is why, for instance, some spirits are still fighting in the battle of Dan-no-Ura (the civil war in Japan in 1185). Their memory of this event has turned into absolute time for them. Some spirits are still fighting for their lives in the battle, whereas others are aware of what happened afterward. Thus, the other world is a world that is strongly based on the subjective view of each spirit.

In the earthly world, there is a certain degree of objectivity; everyone perceives both time and space using the same units. However, that's not how it works in the other world. For example, how you perceive time will be different from the way others perceive it, so once you leave this world, you will start living in a world with various senses of time and space, some of which are completely beyond your understanding.

In the other world, you will undergo a completely different type of soul training than you did in the earthly world. The other world is an incredible world where people have abilities and thoughts beyond imagination. So in order to undergo this new type of soul training, you will need to make further spiritual progress in this world. There are many limitations in the earthly world, but it also has many advantages in terms of the soul's spiritual development. Just as muscles develop under stress from restrictions, our spiritual abilities increase because of the earthly world's limitations.

As I explained, there are opportunities to learn new things in the other world, too. If there weren't, souls would likely be reborn immediately after their earthly life ends. If they return to a realm in the Spirit World where there are no opportunities for new experiences, they would probably be reborn straightaway. But in reality, the other world is a place where souls can gain various experiences, so they stay there for a number of years.

In any case, it's an enjoyable world. Let's meet again in the other world someday.

5

Could You Travel Back in Time in a Time Machine and Change the Past?

Q5

This is a question I have had for a long time. I would like to ask you about the time travel paradox. If one traveled to the past to kill his or her parents, what would happen?

Advanced Level Seminar of 1989, "A Lecture on *The Essence of Buddha*"
Held on October 29, 1989 at Saitama Hall in Saitama, Japan

There are limits to what people from the future can do in the past

The answer to that question is depicted in the movie, *Back to the Future*. The first of the series is already out and the sequel is about to be released (at the time of the lecture), so I am looking forward to seeing what kind of plot it has. Anyhow, as far as I can see from the first movie, there is a premise that the order of cause and effect cannot be changed and that, no matter what you try to change, what is meant to happen will happen. This is how things should be. Otherwise, the order of events will become all jumbled up.

In the Spirit World, too, although there is no time, there is an order of events. You can clearly tell what came before and an event after. We do not know exactly when something happened or will happen, but the order of events exists. The chain of cause and effect is very clear.

Therefore, even if you were able to travel back in time in a time machine, you would not be allowed to tamper with the chain of cause and effect. If you did, you would likely bend and change the laws of the universe, so some kind of force will undoubtedly be at work to prevent that from happening. A force will definitely work to stop you. I myself do not currently know in what way this force will be at work, but if a person from the future traveled back in time and tried to change history, the people of that particular time period—perhaps under the control of heavenly spirits—will try to hinder them from doing so. Such kind of attempt to change history will definitely be under watch. I'm sure that before time travel becomes possible, a moral standard will be established on earth to ensure that these kinds of actions do not take place.

If you look at human history, you can find some records of people who were seemingly from the future. But it is clear that they did not do anything that would change history. The only reason why people from the future are allowed to travel to the past is to indicate the future of humanity in some way. I think this is allowed. People from the future can guide people in a particular age in a good or right direction by suggesting the kind of future they should hope for. However, they probably cannot get directly involved in creating that future. They are limited to making suggestions and nothing more. In this sense, their work is very similar to the work of high spirits and what they can do. This is the extent of what people from the future can do.

The spirits in the other world want to change the earthly world in a certain direction so they send spiritual messages with such hopes, but they never actually use real, physical powers to change this world. This is because doing so would make the existence of this world pointless. If the heavenly spirits were allowed to intervene in this way, there would be no point in people being born into this world as a baby and making efforts as they grow. It would be like putting the cart before the horse.

The spirits could probably intervene if they tried. For example, they could use physical powers to destroy an evil force that appears. This is possible. But that would hinder the soul training that all creatures are undergoing in this autonomous world called the earthly world. Therefore, they are sticking to the policy of "talk the talk but don't walk the walk." Sometimes, a light of angel who is born into this world is killed easily without any resistance. These things occur because the spirits in heaven are sticking to their policy of "keeping their hands off." I'm sure they have the ability to crush the evildoer to save the angel, but they let the situation unfold naturally. This is because there is a rule that prohibits interference, and breaking this rule is an unforgivable act. But sometimes, they are permitted to bring about supernatural phenomena to prove that the Spirit World exists. This is allowed, but I believe they are prohibited from changing any general principles.

So, the same applies to your question. There is probably a higher-ranking god that is in charge of matters like that. Among the higher beings, there is a god who is in charge of time. The spirits in charge of prophecies might also be involved, but there is a god in charge of time, so there must be Laws regarding time. I cannot teach you these Laws at this point in time. But when the time comes for people to use time machines, they will need to learn about these Laws. They might be taught things like "This is the Truth and it must not be bent. You must explore Right Mind. Right Mind means you must not go and tamper with the past." But I think the teachings of this level will be taught in another era.

That is all I can say for now.

CHAPTER FIVE

Understanding the Love and Mercy of God and Buddha

1

The Mistaken Claims Made by Buddhist Scholars Regarding Shakyamuni Buddha

Q1

Right now, I believe that Happy Science is aiming to establish a spiritual perspective of life, which is based on the idea that the spiritual world exists. But on the other hand, I heard that Buddha did not speak about the unconfirmed worlds, namely the spiritual world. Could you please explain in detail why there are different approaches to teaching the Laws?

Special Public Seminar, "Heaven and Hell"
Held on April 26, 1992 at Sendai Sunplaza in Miyagi, Japan

How the Buddhist scholars view Shakyamuni

Many scholars who write books on Buddhism say that Shakyamuni did not teach about spiritual matters. After all, they think that Buddha taught his teachings solely as a philosophy.

Buddhist scholars in Europe are more extreme in their thinking and go as far as to say, "Shakyamuni was an atheist.

He preached atheism and denied God." To them, the word *God* refers to the God in Christianity, which is a monotheistic religion. Shakyamuni, of course, did not teach about such a God, so perhaps he is seen as a denier of God. Some religious scholars even say that Shakyamuni was an atheist, and in a sense, a materialist.

I have actually discussed further on this topic in the May (1992) issue of the Happy Science monthly magazine, which features one of my lectures titled, "What Is Egolessness?" (Compiled in *The Challenge of Enlightenment* [New York: IRH Press, 2022]). The point I wanted to make after all is that there is no way that Shakyamuni could have taught that many sutras if he had known nothing about the other world. He was able to give that many teachings because he received guidance from the other world. However, people didn't start compiling the sutras until at least 300 years after Shakyamuni died, and some were compiled up to 500 years after he died. So, by that time, the teachings that had been

The Challenge of Enlightenment (New York: IRH Press, 2022)

handed down were speculative and could not have been accurate. What's more, the sutras were written based on the level of understanding of the people who compiled them. All of this brought down the spiritual level of Buddha's original teachings.

The same thing can be said of other texts such as Confucius' teachings, and also philosophical texts. There was a philosopher who said, "All of Western philosophy is but a footnote to Plato." What this means is that Western philosophy is nothing more than an elaboration of Plato's thought. But you will not understand the gist of Plato's thought even if you read those philosophies. You simply won't. In the end, people who have not had spiritual experiences will not understand what Plato was trying to convey.

Shakyamuni taught the teachings that a person needed the most

Therefore, the fundamental argument that Shakyamuni did not teach or speak about the other world is false.

It is recorded in Buddhist scriptures that Shakyamuni did not answer 14 metaphysical questions, which are known as the unanswerable questions (*avyakrta* [Sanskrit]). But the correct interpretation is that he did not give answers because even if he did, the person who asked the questions would not have understood them. Shakyamuni was asked many questions like, "Is the universe finite?" "Is there an end to a soul?" "Will we continue to exist after death?" But he did not answer these questions because he thought there was no point in doing so. The person was still at a level where they needed to be taught things like, "You need to study self-reflection," "You need to get up early in the morning," "You need to repent deeply toward your parents," or "You need to make time to read a book every day." He simply did not answer because the person who asked such questions was not ready to learn those kinds of macro-teachings. In this way, Shakyamuni gave various teachings to various people in accordance with what each person needed, and those teachings spread. So what the current Buddhist scholars are doing is citing teachings that Buddha gave to a particular person and making a general statement that he did not answer metaphysical or idealistic questions, or talk about the other world.

However, back in India during Shakyamuni's time, believing in the afterlife was common sense. Reincarnation was also common knowledge. Everyone knew about these things, so they did not need to be brought up. There would be nothing new in teaching about them. That is why

Shakyamuni taught people, "Instead of being concerned about things you already know, first, practice the Four Noble Truths and the Eightfold Path. Stop being distracted and just focus on practicing the teachings." This is what he meant. So the situation in India back then was different from that of Japan today—the other world was a common idea and common knowledge. There was no need to bring it up because it was something as simple as elementary school-level knowledge. The new teachings of Buddha were that people should train themselves by studying and practicing the Four Noble Truths and the Eightfold Path. This was what made Shakyamuni's teachings so distinct from other teachings.

Therefore, to say that Shakyamuni did not teach about the Spirit World is absolutely wrong. The truth is that, during Shakyamuni's time, the existence of the Spirit World was not even in question. Modern-day scholars have no understanding of this.

As a side note, if you ever come across religious scholars, ask them whether they believe in the other world. I would be amazed if even half of them said "Yes." Most of them will respond with a blank stare. But since they still make a living despite being clueless about the other world, they will be going to hell for fraud.

2

The Truth about the Seven Buddhas of the Past

Q2

There is something called "the Seven Buddhas of the Past," which has to do with Shakyamuni's reincarnations. I would appreciate it if you could explain this in more detail.

A Special Public Seminar in Commemoration of the
First Turning of the Wheel of Truth, "What Is the Spirit of Buddhism?"
Held on November 23, 1992 at Tomakomai Civic Hall in Hokkaido, Japan

Buddha's past lives in the Jataka Tales: true or false?

I heard that several people had asked similar questions to yours. To be frank, the Seven Buddhas of the Past are not the same as the past lives of Buddha that we talk about at Happy Science. In truth, these past Buddhas are mere Buddhist traditions. This got mixed up with Shakyamuni Buddha's sermons about his past lives, and are now known as the Seven Buddhas of the Past. This is the reality.

A collection of Buddhist stories called the Jataka Tales tells stories about the various past lives of Shakyamuni. But in reality, those stories are far from the truth. Some of them say that Shakyamuni was once an animal, and others are mostly about things that a bodhisattva did in a city called Benares (now Varanasi). All of the stories are set in India and they follow the same pattern: A person born into a noble class, just like Shakyamuni, decided to leave home to become a monk, underwent discipline, and attained enlightenment. So, they are all stories of virtue.

The truth is that the stories told in the Jataka Tales are a combination of Buddhist folklore, stories about Buddhas that came before Shakyamuni, and other tales that his later disciples wrote. So, to sum up, the names of Shakyamuni's past lives that have been passed down to this day are false. Shakyamuni did not have those past lives.

In reality, just as we teach at Happy Science, Shakyamuni's past lives are Hermes, Rient Arl Croud, and others. Hermes was born in Greece more than 4,000 years ago, Croud was born in the Andes about 6,000 to 7,000 years ago, and Ophealis, who is one of his secret past lives, was also born in Greece. If we go back further in time, Shakyamuni was born in Atlantis about 12,000 years ago and he was called Thoth, and before that, he was born as Ra Mu. This is the truth, but of course, there was no way that people living in India 2,500 to 2,600 years ago would be able to believe that. That is why Shakyamuni set his stories about his past lives in India, and he taught many times that great Buddhas also existed in the past. So the stories about Shakyamuni's past lives are a jumbled mix of his own past lives as well as existing folklore about ancient saints who had attained enlightenment.

In my book, *The Challenge of Enlightenment*, I mentioned the Seven Buddhas of the past, but they do not correspond to Buddha's past lives taught at Happy Science. Back then in India, the Seven Buddhas was simply a Buddhist tradition that said there were six Buddhas before Shakyamuni.

So strictly speaking, the Seven Buddhas of the past do not correspond exactly with Shakyamuni's past lives. The Buddhist stories that are told today are a mix of Shakyamuni's sermons about his past lives and the stories he told people about how there were also figures in the past who taught great Laws.

I have researched each of the six Buddhas before Shakyamuni, but none of them actually existed, so it seems that they are nothing more than folktales. I advise you not to inquire any further about this.

3

Hermes' Love and Jesus' Love with Respect to the Developmental Stages of Love

Q3

You once said, "The Kansai region is similar to the way Greece was in Hermes' time." On the other hand, I heard that you are receiving spiritual assistance from Jesus Christ in today's lecture. With these things in mind, could you teach us more about the difference between the love of Hermes and the love of Jesus?

The Third Public Grand Lecture of 1990, "Be Infinitely Kind"
Held on April 22, 1990 at Kobe Port Island Hall in Hyogo, Japan

Love itself is universal, but the difference lies in the viewpoint from which love is taught

In *The Laws of the Sun*, there is a section about the Theory on the Developmental Stages of Love. You may have already read it, but in that section, I talked about how love—which has been considered a horizontal concept until now—can also be explained as a vertical concept. In other words,

I taught that love comes in stages and that the stages correspond with the stages of enlightenment that a person goes through.

Jesus' love and Hermes' love do not differ in the sense that they are both love. However, they do have a difference in nuance. Hermes' love belongs to the vertical concept of love and is similar to mercy. In other words, his love is largely the love of a great leader. It is strongly characterized by love that guides others as a leader. On the other hand, Jesus' love emphasizes the importance of standing on the same level as others and loving them as fellow human beings. But in truth, love itself is universal and it does not have a vertical or horizontal quality to begin with. The only difference lies in the point of emphasis, how love is taught, and the viewpoint from which love is taught. Some people understand love as mercy that flows from high to low. Others understand love for the first time when it is taught by someone on a similar footing. Either way, it is a matter of how people are guided. This is the difference between Hermes' love and Jesus' love.

The love of Jesus is a type of love where the teacher stands in a relatively similar position to the students. He puts himself in the other person's shoes; he feels their sorrow and suffering as if they were his own. That is his way of giving love. In contrast, Hermes' love is more like the love of a hero. I can only express it using words like these, but I think you can understand the nuances of what I am trying to say.

At any rate, the two are no different in that they are both forms of selfless love. They are both forms of love that pass by like the blowing wind.

4

Hermes' Teachings that Zeus Inherited

Q4

Today, we learned about Hermes' teachings on love and progress. Centuries after Hermes' time, Zeus appeared in Greece and taught about the liberation of human nature. Which part of Hermes' teachings did Zeus inherit and what kind of love did he teach?

The Fourth Public Lecture of 1989, "The Ultimate Self-Realization"
Held on July 8, 1989 at Sonic City in Saitama, Japan

Zeus inherited the spirit of freedom and encouraged each individual to develop their talents

OK, sure. This is a good question.

I spoke about love [in the lecture part] and, in answer to the previous question [of the same Q&A session], I said that love and freedom are closely related to each other.

The main point of love that Hermes taught was that "each person must take action." He taught people to exercise their freedom to the fullest to get closer to God. This teaching spread the spirit of freedom across all of Greece.

Several hundred years later, Zeus came down and inherited Hermes' spirit of freedom, but his focus was on the liberation of human nature through arts and literature. Rather than just focusing on love, Zeus taught people to exercise their freedom to develop their talents and let them blossom in every possible way. He wanted to remove the restrictions on human beings and let their talents freely develop in this world. What's more, he believed that this way of living was in tune with God's Will. He believed that God wished for humans to express all of their talents to their fullest. So, while Hermes' idea of freedom was mainly focused on love, Zeus' idea of freedom was to accept the versatile personalities and abilities of people and let them blossom in their own way.

I am not saying that one teaching is better than the other. Both are important. As I mentioned above, that was how Zeus inherited Hermes' spirit of freedom, which is what led to the development of the arts and the prosperity of Greece during Zeus' time.

5

King Croud of the Ancient Incan Empire and His Involvement with Space Beings

Q5

My question is related to the interaction between human beings and space beings. You have taught us that all kinds of things happened during Rient Arl Croud's time, about 7,000 years ago in South America. Please tell us more about what happened then.

September Seminar of 1989, "Studying the Principle of Wisdom"
Held on September 15, 1989 at the Grand Hotel Hamamatsu in Shizuoka, Japan

King Croud rejected the mass immigration of space beings to Earth

Right now, I am writing a story about the life of Hermes in the Happy Science Monthly Magazine. So I am currently working on "Greek mythology," but I would also like to write about Thoth's time in Atlantis, as well as Ra Mu's time in the Mu Empire, which I presume will be more popular. I would like to tell you about the Incan Empire, too, after people lose interest in these two. In any case, I will teach you about the grand story of Croud's time on a different occasion.

For now, let me just tell you that many space beings visited Earth in Croud's time. As written in *The Laws of the Sun*, there were several occasions on which space beings immigrated to Earth en masse. Due to the negative effect that this had on the population of Earth, there was much discussion among the high spirits in the Real World about whether further migration from other planets was desirable. So, while there was a plan for the mass immigration of space beings during Croud's time, it was rejected in the end.

In the history of Earth, there were several migrations of large spirit groups from other planets. However, this did not increase the spiritual level of the Earth spirit group. Rather, the increase in the population of spirits led to a decrease in its spiritual level. By accepting multiple spirit groups from other planets, the spiritual level of the Earth spirit group dropped, which led to much disorder. These migrations also contributed to the expansion of hell. For this reason, although there was some talk about accepting another mass migration of spirits during Croud's time, the high spirits in the Real World rejected it.

Although the high spirits rejected such an immigration plan, a lot of chaos occurred around that time. During Croud's time, many people in the Incan Empire worshiped space beings as gods. They believed that refusing the wishes of space beings to come to Earth went against God's Will.

So at that time, the Incan Empire was in a civil war-like state over this matter of faith.

At that time, however, Croud began to teach people the following: "The God we believe in is the God that lives in our minds. It is the God that connects to our minds. This is our God." In this way, he clearly taught his people that a god that does not connect to our minds is not God. He struck a blow against people's belief that gods are those who are culturally superior, who have arrived from unknown celestial bodies, or who have advanced technology. He denounced the idea completely and said, "That is wrong. Those who are connected to the teachings of the mind, in other words, those who wish to nurture others and make them happy are the ones who are close to God. The level of culture or science alone does not determine whether one is God."

Although people were perplexed by his teachings, he managed to bring order to them. This is the simple version of the story of Croud's time. I hope to tell you a much larger-scale version of it at another time.

6

Awakening to the Great Love of God

Q6

Despite all of us being embraced by Master Ryuho Okawa's great love, we have been so dependent on you that the activities we have carried out are so feeble. I think we are responsible for making you shed tears during your first lecture this year at Makuhari Messe titled, "Faith and Love." Today, I would like to take this opportunity on behalf of all your disciples to apologize sincerely and make a new vow.

We, disciples, promise you that we will give it our all and make our utmost efforts to definitely create a wonderful world. Please watch over us from now on. We will do our best to assist you. Thank you very much.

The Third Public Grand Lecture of 1990, "Be Infinitely Kind"
Held on April 22, 1990 at Kobe Port Island Hall in Hyogo, Japan

Not offering the Truth to people who are lost is a sin on our half

OK. Well, this is not a question, but let me respond to your words since you are so passionate.

Today, many people have gathered in the Kansai region. Last year, over 3,000 people gathered, but today, I think we have a full house (8,000 people). It makes me very happy. Since I am not able to give many public lectures in Kansai each year, I hope you seize the chance to attend one when I do.

About ten years ago, I myself was just like everyone else and did not give much thought to the Truth. I believe that many people here today are also like that. What they need is an opportunity to awaken to the Truth. Although it is up to each individual whether to awaken or not, it is our job to offer them the opportunity to do so. It is my job and it is also the job of all Happy Science members. In fact, this is our most important job.

Please give the opportunity to learn the Truth to as many people as possible. Today's lecture (titled "Be Infinitely Kind") was about family, so I did not talk about the all-encompassing Laws. But ultimately, being infinitely kind means conveying the Truth to people. This is because many people do not know about the Truth. They have the potential to awaken, but because they don't know the Truth, they cannot. What is more, many people are living under wrong teachings, with wrong ideas, and under mistaken religions. This is truly heartbreaking. If these people leave this world without a chance to learn about the Truth despite us carrying out our activities during the same age, it is something we must truly repent for. It is a sin on their half for being lost, but it is a sin on our half if we do not give them the opportunity to learn the Truth. These people can definitely encounter the Truth as long as our members on earth make efforts to offer it to them.

Plant the seeds of Truth in return for the love you received

The high spirits are sending us messages of overflowing passion. The ones to receive and act on these messages are we, the humans who are alive. We must give back.

We talk about "love that gives," but essentially, we have already been given everything. So being kind to others is our duty and a natural course of action. To be awakened to the Truth means to be aware of how much love you have been receiving from God. When you are aware of this, you will naturally want to give back. This is what it means to plant the seeds of Truth.

Please carry out your activities with a pure heart. In this world, all kinds of religions exist, so people may assume that you belong to a mistaken religion and criticize you. You may be hurt by their comments.

But I say to you: What we teach is the Truth. The teachings of Happy Science are the Truth. They are definitely right. I am fully convinced of that.

Afterword

There is a Buddhist term, *taiki-seppo*, which means to preach Buddha's Truth according to the spiritual level of the listener. This is indeed very difficult to do, so in a sense, being able to do so is proof of being Buddha.

By reading all seven volumes of the Q&A series many times, you will be versed in all the secrets of life. Now that Happy Science has become a massive religious group, I am unable to answer each question people have. Therefore, I believe this book will take on more and more value as time goes on.

For the people who are striving to convey the Truth to others, my early lectures series and Q&A sessions series are absolutely necessary learning materials.

There will come a day when you can only learn Buddha's words through writing.

I sincerely hope that you will savor the significance of living in this present age.

Ryuho Okawa
Master & CEO of Happy Science Group
February 11, 2022

For a deeper understanding of
The Truth about Earth, the Universe, the Spirit World:
Life's Q&A with El Cantare
see other books below by Ryuho Okawa:

The Laws of the Sun [New York: IRH Press, 2018]

The Golden Laws [Tokyo: HS Press, 2015]

The Laws of Eternity [New York: IRH Press, 2024]

An Unshakable Mind [New York: IRH Press, 2023]

The Ten Principles from El Cantare Volume 1 [New York: IRH Press, 2021]

The Challenge of Enlightenment [New York: IRH Press, 2022]

ABOUT THE AUTHOR

Founder and CEO of Happy Science Group.

Ryuho Okawa was born on July 7th, 1956, in Tokushima, Japan. After graduating from the University of Tokyo with a law degree, he joined a Tokyo-based trading company. While working at its New York headquarters, he studied international finance at the Graduate Center of the City University of New York. In 1981, he attained Great Enlightenment and became aware that he is El Cantare with a mission to bring salvation to all humankind.

In 1986, he established Happy Science. It now has members in 180 countries across the world, with more than 700 branches and temples as well as 10,000 missionary houses around the world.

He has given over 3,500 lectures (of which more than 150 are in English) and published over 3,200 books (of which more than 600 are Spiritual Interview Series), and many are translated into 42 languages. Along with *The Laws of the Sun* and *The Laws of Hell*, many of the books have become best sellers or million sellers. To date, Happy Science has produced 28 movies under his supervision. He has given the original story and concept and is also the Executive Producer. He has also composed music and written lyrics for over 450 pieces.

Moreover, he is the Founder of Happy Science University and Happy Science Academy (Junior and Senior High School), Founder and President of the Happiness Realization Party, Founder and Honorary Headmaster of Happy Science Institute of Government and Management, Founder of IRH Press Co., Ltd., and the Chairperson of NEW STAR PRODUCTION Co., Ltd. and ARI Production Co., Ltd.

BOOKS BY RYUHO OKAWA

The Laws Series

The Laws of the Sun, the first publication of the Laws Series, ranked in the annual best-selling list in Japan in 1994. After that, the Laws series' titles had always been ranked in the annual best-selling list, setting socio-cultural trends in Japan and around the world. The first three Laws series are *The Laws of the Sun*, *The Golden Laws*, and *The Laws of Eternity*.

The Laws of the Sun

One Source, One Planet, One People

Paperback • 288 pages • $15.95
ISBN: 978-1-942125-43-3 (Oct. 25, 2018)

IMAGINE IF YOU COULD ASK GOD why He created this world and about the spiritual laws He used to shape us and everything around us. If we could understand His designs and intentions, we could discover what our goals in life should be and whether our actions move us closer to those goals or farther away.

At a young age, a spiritual calling prompted Ryuho Okawa to outline what he innately understood to be universal truths for all humankind. In *The Laws of the Sun*, Okawa outlines these laws of the universe and provides a road map for living one's life with greater purpose and meaning. In this powerful book, Ryuho Okawa reveals the transcendent nature of consciousness and the secrets of the multidimensional universe as well as the meaning of humans that exist within it. By understanding the different stages of love and following the Buddhist Eightfold Path, he believes we can speed up our eternal process of development. *The Laws of the Sun* shows the way to realize true happiness—a happiness that continues from this world through the other.

The Laws of Eternity

El Cantare Unveils the Structure of the Spirit World

Paperback • 224 pages • $17.95
ISBN: 978-1-958655-16-0 (May 15, 2024)

"Where do we come from and where do we go after death?"

This unparalleled book offers us complete answers to life's most important questions that we all are confronted with at some point or another. In *The Laws of Eternity*, author Ryuho Okawa takes us on a journey to the other world, a place where we came from before we were born and return to after death.

This book reveals the eternal mysteries and the ultimate secrets of Earth's spirit group that have been covered by the veil of legends and myths. Encountering the long-hidden Eternal Truths that are revealed for the first time in human history will change the way you live your life now.

Recommended Books

The Truth about Spiritual Phenomena

Life's Q&A with El Cantare

Paperback • 232 pages • $17.95
ISBN: 978-1-958655-0-92 (Oct. 27, 2023)

These are the records of Ryuho Okawa's answers to 26 questions related to spiritual phenomena and mental health, which were conducted live during his early public lectures with the audience. With his great spiritual ability, he revealed the unknown spiritual Truth behind the spiritual phenomena.

The Mystical Laws

Going Beyond the Dimensional Boundaries

Paperback • 252 pages • $14.95
ISBN: 979-8-887370-3-85 (Mar. 5, 2015)

"No matter how much you suffer, the Truth will gradually shine forth as you continue to endure hardships. Therefore, simply strengthen your mind and keep making constant efforts in times of endurance, however ordinary they may be. "

-From Postscript

The Laws of Hell

"IT" follows.....

Paperback • 264 pages • $17.95
ISBN: 978-1-958655-04-7 (May 1, 2023)

Whether you believe it or not, the Spirit World and hell do exist, and unfortunately, 1 in 2 people are falling to hell. To stop hell from spreading and to save the souls of all human beings, Ryuho Okawa has compiled vital teachings in this book. This publication marks his 3,100th book and is the one and only comprehensive Truth about the modern hell.

What Is Happy Science?

Best Selection of Ryuho Okawa's
Early Lectures (Volume 1)

Paperback • 200 pages • $17.95
ISBN: 978-1-942125-99-0 (Aug. 25, 2023)

The Best Selection series is a collection of Ryuho Okawa's passionate lectures from the ages of 32 to 33 that reveal the mission and goal of Happy Science. This book contains the eternal Truth, including the meaning of life, the secret of the mind, the true meaning of love, the mystery of the universe, and how to end hatred and world conflicts.

The Way to Human Perfection

Best Selection of Ryuho Okawa's
Early Lectures (Volume 2)

Paperback • 200 pages • $17.95
ISBN: 978-1-958655-20-7 (Oct. 22, 2024)

The path to enlightenment starts from understanding 'the eternal viewpoint of life.' Through each chapter, Ryuho Okawa navigates us to shift the perspective of ourselves from a 'finite self' living a limited life to an 'eternal self' living an eternal life.

Basic Teachings of Happy Science

The Ten Principles from El Cantare Volume I

Ryuho Okawa's First Lectures on His Basic Teachings

Paperback • 232 pages • $16.95
ISBN: 978-1-942125-85-3 (Dec. 15, 2021)

This book contains the historic lectures given on the first five principles of the Ten Principles of Happy Science by the author, Ryuho Okawa, who is revered as World Teacher. These lectures produced an enthusiastic fellowship in Happy Science Japan and became the foundation of the current global utopian movement. You can learn the essence of Okawa's teachings and the secret behind the rapid growth of the Happy Science movement in simple language.

The Ten Principles from El Cantare Volume II

Ryuho Okawa's First Lectures on His Wish to Save the World

Paperback • 216 pages • $16.95
ISBN: 978-1-942125-86-0 (May 3, 2022)

A sequel to *The Ten Principles from El Cantare Volume I.* Volume II reveals the Creator's three major inventions; the secret of the creation of human souls, the meaning of time, and 'happiness' as life's purpose. By reading this book, you can not only improve yourself but learn how to make a difference in society and create an ideal, utopian world.

The Laws of Happiness

Love, Wisdom, Self-Reflection
and Progress

Paperback • 264 pages • $16.95
ISBN: 978-1-942125-70-9 (Aug. 28, 2020)

Happiness is not found outside us; it is found within us. It is in how we think, how we look at our lives, and how we devote our hearts to the work we do. Discover how the Fourfold Path of Love, Wisdom, Self-Reflection, and Progress creates a life of sustainable happiness.

Developmental Stages of Love - The Original Theory

Philosophy of Love in My Youth

Hardcover • 200 pages • $17.95
ISBN: 978-1-942125-94-5 (Jun. 15, 2022)

This book is about author Ryuho Okawa's original philosophy of love which serves as the foundation of love in chapter three of *The Laws of the Sun*. It consists of a series of short essays authored during the age of 25 through 28 while he was working as a young promising business elite at an international trading company after attaining the Great Enlightenment in 1981. The developmental stages of love unite love and enlightenment, West and East, and bridge Christianity and Buddhism.

The Latest Titles

One More Step Forward

The Invincible Thinking to get you through tough times

Paperback • 256 pages • $17.95
ISBN: 978-1-958655-25-2 (May 7, 2025)

Success in life is determined not by our circumstances but by our mindset and how we think. In this book, the author reveals from his first-hand experience how the spirit of self-help can create new values.

Ryuho Okawa is a true self-made man with an indomitable spirit to bring happiness to all humankind. His drive to keep moving forward by taking steady steps through the power of discipline has led to the publication of over 3,200 books in just 37 years. Unlock the keys to lifelong growth and success by reading this book.

Words to Stop You from Falling to Hell

Paperback • 136 pages • $15.95
ISBN: 979-8-88737-123-8 (Jan. 27, 2025)

This book serves as both a warning and a guide, offering insights to help us avoid falling into hell in the afterlife. The phrases and descriptions within are based on actual accounts from the author who witnessed these unsettling realities through his profound spiritual perspective.

My Visit to Hell

The Reality of the Underworld Anyone May Face

Paperback • 178 pages • $20.00
ISBN: 979-8-88737-124-5(Feb. 26, 2025)

This book is a shocking account of the current hell the author saw in his spiritual journey. He has been warning that in this increasingly materialistic world, more than half of the population is falling to hell. That is why it is crucial for people to know the causes of humans falling to hell and learn what it means to live righteously.

The Eternal Buddha

Now, Here, Is the Imperishable Light

Hardcover • 200 pages • $17.95
ISBN: 978-1-958655-19-1 (Sep 15, 2024)

This book is a powerful source of guidance for those seeking Truth. Embedded within, you will find the infinite wisdom of the Eternal Buddha and come to realize that you are not just a physical being, but an eternal soul of brilliant light. Through the words of the Eternal Buddha, unlock the boundless treasures of enlightenment given to humankind in this modern era.

Buddhist Teachings for People Today

The Essence of Buddha

The Path to Enlightenment

Paperback • 208 pages • $14.95
ISBN: 978-1-942125-06-8 (Oct. 1, 2016)

The essence of Shakyamuni Buddha's original teachings of the mind are explained in simple words. Through this book, you will learn how to attain inner happiness, the wisdom to conquer ego, and to enter the path to enlightenment. It is a way of life that people in this modern age can practice to achieve lifelong self-growth.

The Challenge of Enlightenment

Now, Here, the New Dharma Wheel Turns

Paperback • 380 pages • $17.95
ISBN: 978-1-942125-92-1 (Dec. 20, 2022)

Buddha's teachings, a reflection of his eternal wisdom, are like a bamboo pole used to change the course of your boat in the rapid stream of the great river called life. By reading this book, your mind becomes clearer and learns to savor inner peace, and you will be empowered to make profound life improvements.

The Challenge of the Mind

An Essential Guide to Buddha's Teachings: Zen, Karma and Enlightenment

Paperback • 208 pages • $16.95
ISBN: 978-1-942125-45-7 (Nov. 15, 2018)

In this book, Ryuho Okawa explains essential Buddhist tenets and how to put them into practice. Enlightenment is not just an abstract idea but one that everyone can experience to some extent. Okawa offers a solid basis of reason and an intellectual understanding of Buddhist concepts.

The Truth about the Spirit World

The Laws Of Messiah

From Love to Love

Paperback • 248 pages • $16.95
ISBN: 978-1-942125-90-7 (Jan. 31, 2022)

"What is Messiah?" This book carries an important message of love and guidance to people living now from the Modern-Day Messiah or the Modern-Day Savior. It also reveals the secret of Shambhala, the spiritual center of Earth, as well as the truth that this spiritual center is currently in danger of perishing and what we can do to protect this sacred place.

My Journey through the Spirit World

A True Account of My Experiences of the Hereafter

Paperback • 224 pages • $15.95
ISBN: 978-1-942125-41-9 (Jul. 25, 2018)

In this book, Ryuho Okawa shares surprising facts about the afterworld. This unique and authentic guide to the Spirit World will awaken us to the truth of life and death, and show us how we should start living so that we can return to a bright world of heaven.

Spiritual World 101

A Guide to a Spiritually Happy Life

Paperback • 184 pages • $14.95
ISBN: 979-8-88737-031-6 (Mar. 25, 2015)

This book is a spiritual guidebook that will answer all your questions about the spiritual world, with illustrations and diagrams explaining your guardian spirit and the secrets of God and Buddha. By reading this book, you will be able to understand the true meaning of life and find happiness in everyday life.

WHO IS EL CANTARE?

El Cantare means "the Light of the Earth." He is the Supreme God of the Earth who has been guiding humankind since the beginning of Genesis, and He is the Creator of the universe. He is whom Jesus called Father and Muhammad called Allah and is *Ame-no-Mioya-Gami*, Japanese Father God. Different parts of El Cantare's core consciousness have descended to Earth in the past, once as Alpha and another as Elohim. His branch spirits, such as Shakyamuni Buddha and Hermes, have descended to Earth many times and helped to flourish many civilizations. To unite various religions and to integrate various fields of study in order to build a new civilization on Earth, a part of the core consciousness has descended to Earth as Master Ryuho Okawa.

Alpha is a part of the core consciousness of El Cantare who descended to Earth around 330 million years ago. Alpha preached Earth's Truths to harmonize and unify Earth-born humans and space people who came from other planets.

Elohim is a part of the core consciousness of El Cantare who descended to Earth around 150 million years ago. He gave wisdom, mainly on the differences between light and darkness, good and evil.

Ame-no-Mioya-Gami (Japanese Father God) is the Creator God and the Father God who appears in ancient literature, *Hotsuma Tsutae*. It is believed that He descended on the foothills of Mt. Fuji about 30,000 years ago and built the Fuji dynasty, which is the root of the Japanese civilization. With justice as the central pillar, Ame-no-Mioya-Gami's teachings spread to ancient civilizations of other countries in the world.

Shakyamuni Buddha was born in Lumbini (now located in Nepal) around 2,600 years ago as the prince of the Shakya clan. When he was 29 years old, he renounced the world and sought enlightenment. He later attained Great Enlightenment in Bodh Gaya, India, and founded Buddhism, which has spread extensively throughout Asia.

Hermes is one of the 12 Olympian gods in Greek mythology, but the spiritual Truth is that he taught the teachings of love and progress around 4,300 years ago which became the origin of the current Western civilization. He is a hero who truly existed.

Ophealis was born in Greece around 6,500 years ago and was the leader who took an expedition to as far as Egypt. He is the God of miracles, prosperity, and arts, and is known as Osiris in Egyptian mythology.

Rient Arl Croud was born as a king of the ancient Incan Empire around 7,000 years ago and taught about the mysteries of the mind. In the heavenly world, he is responsible for the interactions that take place between various planets.

Thoth was an almighty leader who built the golden age of the Atlantic civilization around 12,000 years ago. In Egyptian mythology, he is known as God Thoth.

Ra Mu was a leader who built the golden age of the civilization of Mu around 17,000 years ago. As a religious leader and a politician, he ruled by uniting religion and politics.

ABOUT HAPPY SCIENCE

Happy Science is a religious group founded on the faith in El Cantare who is the God of the Earth, and the Creator of the universe. The essence of human beings is the soul that was created by God, and we all are children of God. God is our true parent, so in our souls, we have a fundamental desire to "believe in God, love God, and get closer to God." And, we can get closer to God by living with God's Will as our own. In Happy Science, we call this the "Exploration of Right Mind." More specifically, it means to practice the Fourfold Path, which consists of "Love, Wisdom, Self-Reflection, and Progress."

Love: Love means "love that gives," or mercy. God hopes for the happiness of all people. Therefore, living with God's Will as our own means to start by practicing "love that gives."

Wisdom: God's love is boundless. It is important to learn various Truths in order to understand the heart of God.

Self-Reflection: Once you learn the heart of God and the difference between His mind and yours, you should strive to bring your own mind closer to the mind of God—that process is called self-reflection. Self-reflection also includes meditation and prayer.

Progress: Since God hopes for the happiness of all people, you should also make progress in your love, and make an effort to realize utopia in which everyone in your society, country, and eventually all humankind can become happy.

As we practice this Fourfold Path, our souls will advance toward God step by step. That is when we can attain real happiness—our souls' desire to get closer to God comes true.

In Happy Science, we conduct activities to make ourselves happy through belief in Lord El Cantare and to spread this faith to the world and bring happiness to all. We welcome you to join our activities!

We hold events and activities to help you practice the Fourfold Path at our branches, temples, missionary centers, and missionary houses

Love: We hold various volunteering activities. Our members conduct missionary work together as the greatest practice of love.

Wisdom: We offer our comprehensive collection of books of Truth, many of which are available online and at Happy Science locations. In addition, we offer numerous opportunities such as seminars or book clubs to learn the Truth.

Self-Reflection: We offer opportunities to polish your mind through self-reflection, meditation, and prayer. Many members have experienced improvement in their human relationships by changing their own minds.

Progress: We also offer seminars to enhance your power of influence. Because it is also important to do well at work to make society better, we hold seminars to improve your work and management skills.

HAPPY SCIENCE'S ENGLISH SUTRA

"The True Words Spoken By Buddha"

"The True Words Spoken By Buddha" is an English sutra given directly from the spirit of Shakyamuni Buddha, who is a part of Master Ryuho Okawa's subconscious. The words in this sutra are not of a mere human being but are the words of God or Buddha sent directly from the ninth dimension, which is the highest realm of the Earth's Spirit World.

"The True Words Spoken By Buddha" is an essential sutra for us to connect and live with God or Buddha's Will as our own.

MEMBERSHIPS

MEMBERSHIP

If you would like to know more about Happy Science, please consider becoming a member. Those who pledge to believe in Lord El Cantare and wish to learn more can join us.

When you become a member, you will receive the following sutras: "The True Words Spoken By Buddha," "Prayer to the Lord" and "Prayer to Guardian and Guiding Spirits."

DEVOTEE MEMBER

If you would like to learn the teachings of Happy Science and walk the path of faith, become a Devotee member who pledges devotion to the Three Treasures, which are Buddha, Dharma, and Sangha. Buddha refers to Lord El Cantare, Master Ryuho Okawa. Dharma refers to Master Ryuho Okawa's teachings. Sangha refers to Happy Science. Devoting to the Three Treasures will let your Buddha nature shine, and you will enter the path to attain true freedom of the mind.

Becoming a devotee means you become Buddha's disciple. You will discipline your mind and act to bring happiness to society.

EMAIL OR **PHONE CALL**

Please turn to the contact information page.

ONLINE member.happy-science.org/signup/

CONTACT INFORMATION

Happy Science is a worldwide organization with branches and temples around the globe. For full details, visit happy-science.org. The following are some of our main Happy Science locations:

United States and Canada

New York
79 Franklin St., New York, NY 10013, USA
Phone: 1-212-343-7972
Fax: 1-212-343-7973
Email: ny@happy-science.org
Website: happyscience-usa.org

New Jersey
66 Hudson St., #2R, Hoboken, NJ 07030, USA
Phone: 1-201-313-0127
Email: nj@happy-science.org
Website: happyscience-usa.org

Chicago
33 West Higgins Rd. 4040,
South Barrington, IL 60010, USA
Phone: 1-630-937-3077
Email: chicago@happy-science.org
Website: happyscience-usa.org

Florida
5208 8th St., Zephyrhills, FL 33542, USA
Phone: 1-813-715-0000
Fax: 1-813-715-0010
Email: florida@happy-science.org
Website: happyscience-usa.org

Atlanta
1874 Piedmont Ave., NE Suite 360-C
Atlanta, GA 30324, USA
Phone: 1-404-892-7770
Email: atlanta@happy-science.org
Website: happyscience-usa.org

San Francisco
525 Clinton St.
Redwood City, CA 94062, USA
Phone & Fax: 1-650-363-2777
Email: sf@happy-science.org
Website: happyscience-usa.org

Los Angeles
1590 E. Del Mar Blvd., Pasadena,
CA 91106, USA
Phone: 1-626-395-7775
Fax: 1-626-395-7776
Email: la@happy-science.org
Website: happyscience-usa.org

Orange County
16541 Gothard St. Suite 104
Huntington Beach, CA 92647
Phone: 1-714-659-1501
Email: oc@happy-science.org
Website: happyscience-usa.org

San Diego
7841 Balboa Ave. Suite #202
San Diego, CA 92111, USA
Phone: 1-626-395-7775
Fax: 1-626-395-7776
E-mail: sandiego@happy-science.org
Website: happyscience-usa.org

Hawaii
Phone: 1-808-591-9772
Fax: 1-808-591-9776
Email: hi@happy-science.org
Website: happyscience-usa.org

Kauai
3343 Kanakolu Street, Suite 5
Lihue, HI 96766, USA
Phone: 1-808-822-7007
Fax: 1-808-822-6007
Email: kauai-hi@happy-science.org
Website: happyscience-usa.org

Toronto
845 The Queensway
Etobicoke, ON, M8Z 1N6, Canada
Phone: 1-416-901-3747
Email: toronto@happy-science.org
Website: happy-science.ca

Vancouver
#201-2607 East 49th Avenue,
Vancouver, BC, V5S 1J9, Canada
Phone: 1-604-437-7735
Fax: 1-604-437-7764
Email: vancouver@happy-science.org
Website: happy-science.ca

INTERNATIONAL

Tokyo
1-6-7 Togoshi, Shinagawa,
Tokyo, 142-0041, Japan
Phone: 81-3-6384-5770
Fax: 81-3-6384-5776
Email: tokyo@happy-science.org
Website: happy-science.org

London
3 Margaret St.
London, W1W 8RE United Kingdom
Phone: 44-20-7323-9255
Fax: 44-20-7323-9344
Email: eu@happy-science.org
Website: www.happyscience-uk.org

Sydney
516 Pacific Highway, Lane Cove North,
2066 NSW, Australia
Phone: 61-2-9411-2877
Fax: 61-2-9411-2822
Email: sydney@happy-science.org

Sao Paulo
Rua. Domingos de Morais 1154,
Vila Mariana, Sao Paulo SP
CEP 04010-100, Brazil
Phone: 55-11-5088-3800
Email: sp@happy-science.org
Website: happyscience.com.br

Jundiai
Rua Congo, 447, Jd. Bonfiglioli
Jundiai-CEP, 13207-340, Brazil
Phone: 55-11-4587-5952
Email: jundiai@happy-science.org

Seoul
74, Sadang-ro 27-gil,
Dongjak-gu, Seoul, Korea
Phone: 82-2-3478-8777
Fax: 82-2-3478-9777
Email: korea@happy-science.org

Taipei
No. 89, Lane 155, Dunhua N. Road,
Songshan District, Taipei City 105, Taiwan
Phone: 886-2-2719-9377
Fax: 886-2-2719-5570
Email: taiwan@happy-science.org

Taichung
No. 146, Minzu Rd., Central Dist.,
Taichung City 400001, Taiwan
Phone: 886-4-22233777
Email: taichung@happy-science.org

Kuala Lumpur
No 22A, Block 2, Jalil Link Jalan Jalil Jaya
2, Bukit Jalil 57000,
Kuala Lumpur, Malaysia
Phone: 60-3-8998-7877
Fax: 60-3-8998-7977
Email: malaysia@happy-science.org
Website: happyscience.org.my

Kathmandu
Kathmandu Metropolitan City,
Ward No. 15, Ring Road, Kimdol,
Sitapaila Kathmandu, Nepal
Phone: 977-1-537-2931
Email: nepal@happy-science.org

Kampala
Plot 877 Rubaga Road, Kampala
P.O. Box 34130 Kampala, Uganda
Email: uganda@happy-science.org

ABOUT HAPPINESS REALIZATION PARTY

The Happiness Realization Party (HRP) was founded in May 2009 by Master Ryuho Okawa as part of the Happy Science Group. HRP strives to improve Japanese society, based on three basic political principles of "freedom, democracy, and faith," and let Japan promote individual and public happiness from Asia to the world as a leader nation.

1) Diplomacy and Security: Protecting Freedom, Democracy, and Faith of Japan and the World from China's Totalitarianism

Japan's current defense system is insufficient against China's expanding hegemony and the threat of North Korea's nuclear missiles. Japan, as the leader of Asia, must strengthen its defense power and promote strategic diplomacy together with the nations that share the values of freedom, democracy, and faith. Further, HRP aims to realize world peace under the leadership of Japan, a nation with the spirit of religious tolerance.

2) Economy: Early economic recovery through utilizing the "wisdom of the private sector"

The economy has been damaged severely since the outbreak of the novel coronavirus originated in China. Many companies have been forced into bankruptcy or out of business. What is needed for economic recovery now is not subsidies and regulations by the government, but policies that can utilize the "wisdom of the private sector."

For more information, visit en.hr-party.jp

HAPPY SCIENCE ACADEMY JUNIOR AND SENIOR HIGH SCHOOL

Happy Science Academy Junior and Senior High School is a boarding school founded with the goal of educating the future leaders of the world who can have a big vision, persevere, and take on new challenges.

Currently, there are two campuses in Japan; the Nasu Main Campus in Tochigi Prefecture, founded in 2010, and the Kansai Campus in Shiga Prefecture, founded in 2013.

HAPPY SCIENCE UNIVERSITY

THE FOUNDING SPIRIT AND THE GOAL OF EDUCATION

Based on the founding philosophy of the university, "Exploration of happiness and the creation of a new civilization," education, research, and studies will be provided to help students acquire a deep understanding grounded in religious belief and advanced expertise with the objectives of producing "great talents of virtue" who can contribute in a broad-ranging way to serve Japan and the international society.

FACULTIES

Faculty of human happiness

Students in this faculty will pursue liberal arts from various perspectives with a multidisciplinary approach, explore and envision an ideal state of human beings and society.

Faculty of successful management

This faculty aims to realize successful management that helps organizations create value and wealth for society and to contribute to the happiness and development of management and employees as well as society as a whole.

Faculty of future creation

Students in this faculty study subjects such as political science, journalism, performing arts, and artistic expression, and explore and present new political and cultural models based on truth, goodness, and beauty.

Faculty of future industry

This faculty aims to nurture engineers who can resolve various issues facing modern civilization from a technological standpoint and contribute to the creation of new industries of the future.

ABOUT IRH PRESS USA INC.

Founded in 2013, New York-based IRH Press USA Inc. is the North American affiliate of IRH Press Co., Ltd., Japan. The Press exclusively publishes comprehensive titles on Spiritual Truth, religious enrichment, Buddhism, personal growth, and contemporary commentary by Ryuho Okawa, the author of more than 3,200 unique publications, with hundreds of millions of copies sold worldwide. For more information, visit Okawabooks.com.

Follow us on:

- Facebook: Okawa Books
- Youtube: Okawa Books
- Pinterest: Okawa Books
- Instagram: OkawaBooks
- Twitter: Okawa Books
- Goodreads: Ryuho Okawa

NEWSLETTER

To receive book-related news, promotions and events, please subscribe to our newsletter below.

irhpress.com/pages/subscribe

AUDIO / VISUAL MEDIA

YOUTUBE

PODCAST

Visit the above to learn more about Ryuho Okawa's books. Topics range from self-help, current affairs, spirituality, religion, and the universe.